Beyond the Box:

Lean Out, Break Free, Rise Up!

by

Judith Rich, Ph.D.

Rise Up!
Best wishes
Judith Rich

Published by Best Seller Publishing®, Pasadena, CA
Best Seller Publishing® is a registered trademark
Printed in the United States of America.

ISBN: 978-1-946978-78-3

This publication is designed to provide accurate and authoritative information with regard to the subject matter covered. It is sold with the understanding that the publisher is not engaged in rendering legal, accounting, or other professional advice. If legal advice or other expert assistance is required, the services of a competent professional should be sought. The opinions expressed by the authors in this book are not endorsed by Best Seller Publishing® and are the sole responsibility of the author rendering the opinion.

Most Best Seller Publishing® titles are available at special quantity discounts for bulk purchases for sales promotions, premiums, fundraising, and educational use. Special versions or book excerpts can also be created to fit specific needs.

For more information, please write:
Best Seller Publishing®
1346 Walnut Street, #205
Pasadena, CA 91106
or call 1(626) 765 9750
Toll Free: 1(844) 850-3500
Visit us online at: www.BestSellerPublishing.org

Testimonials

"Judith Rich brings three quarters of a century of wisdom, experience and fiery passion to anyone out there with a calling and a knowing there is more of life to explore. I have known Dr. Rich for over 25 years, and worked with her on stage, shared the pages of the Huffington Post as thought leadership columnists, and watched her travel the globe touching tens of thousands of lives. Dr. Rich walks her talk. She thinks deeply, she lives from her values, and she is fiercely committed to her path. She will serve as your provocateur, and cajole you to find the courage you never thought you had, followed by a kick in the pants to leap into greatness. I have no doubt parts of this book will grip the edges of your deepest fears, call you out on your old stories (bullshit), nudge you into a new thought pattern, and catapult into action with the confidence of a super hero. Read this book. Read it all - you can thank me later."

–Kari Henley, Founder, Age Without Borders
www.agewoborders.com - Fort Collins, CO.

"I have known Judith Rich for 44 years. She walks her talk. Truly, she should be on America's national treasure list. Having inspired literally thousands of students here and abroad, she is a life-changer, gifted writer, mother and grandmother as well. Just how she fits this all in is a wonder, indeed. Readers will meet a new, beloved friend and coach in her. Their lives will open in profound ways!

Her book is especially important for anyone who is sincere in wanting to expand what matters most in life."

–**Dr. Cara Lee Barker**, Jungian Analyst, Zurich Diplomate
Author of World Weary Woman: Her Wound and Transformation:
and The Love Project
www.carabarker.com- Kirkland, WA.

"Let's be real. We are living through trying times. Our nervous systems need all the support we can muster to keep us encouraged, evolving, and hopeful.

Based on years of experience, **Beyond the Box**, grabs us in the deepest parts of our knowing, holding on tight, inviting us to become, what is already uniquely ours.

It is an invitation for these times, an appropriate response, calling us to illuminate our spiritual wisdom light, that waits to sparkle with passion and truth, in service for us all."

–**Ronita Johnson**, Convener "Women Eradicating Racism"
& "The Millionth Circle", Author "Coming To Forgiveness: A Daughter's
Story of Race, Rage & Religion" and Solo Performer "FORGIVEABLE".
www.comingtoforgiveness.com

"Judith Rich represents what is needed in a despairing world – – a GENUINE OPTIMIST, whose point of view is grounded in deep intelligence, commitment and experience.

Judith is a rare, pure-hearted leader. Her authenticity and expansive generosity motivate her, again and again, to continually transform the consciousness of the planet – –one action, one thought and one commitment at a time. It is a privilege to share in her inspired wisdom.

–**Eleanor Hanauer** Transformational trainer, coach and speaker
Mill Valley, CA.

"Dr. Judith Rich is committed to service and transformation. Her lifework as a personal and leadership development trainer and coach has touched thousands and is evidence of her calling and faithful response. Her book extends her reach and capacity to serve more of us in a guided process of awakening to our calling and making a positive difference on the planet. Her generous contribution gives us access to practical advice and a manual for upgrading our lives.

+Judith sees us for who we are, calls us out and supports our growth and development. Her book is both a breath of fresh air and a call to illuminate the darkness with our inner light. Through very specific practices, we learn how to transmute chaos and build a bold new life. Just in the nick of time!"

–**Reverend Andriette Earl**, author, Embracing Wholeness:
Living in Spiritual Congruence
Senior and Founding Minister,
Heart and Soul Center of Light - Oakland, California
www.heartsoulcenter.org

"Beyond The Box reflects the soul and purpose of Judith Rich. Hers is calling to support others to find and live their true calling. My soul wanted to break free of the Box and hear my inner calling and purpose as I was reading it. Judith has been an important mentor for me and for the people of México who seek to find their true purpose. A wise soul waking up other young souls like mine. A light in the darkness."

–**Erik Esparza**, transformational trainer and interpreter
Mexico City, Mexico

"Dr. Judith Rich has always been a warrior in this world. I first met her in 1999 and she had already worked as a trainer in the experiential learning business over 30 years. She stepped into the human development waves in her thirty's and stood on the front line to meet the changes all those years. She brought inspiration to people in any scenario. Every few years I talked to her and was always amazed how her thinking and attitudes were ahead of most of people.

I am so glad for this book to be published. It contains the core values and practices that Dr. Rich represents. It is crucial to have a coach, a mentor to talk to when one's personal path is unfolding and vision being manifested. Judith shares her heart, her experiences and her professional abilities to guide us on this most important journey in our life. It is a book that will be valuable for a lifetime."

–**Phiona Chung**, musician, teacher, adventurer, interpreter
Taipai, Taiwan

"I've known Judith for over 11 years and her words are pure magic. She's broken more people through to success then anyone I know. If you come across this book consider it a prayer answered and you should stop everything and read it now! Then share it with someone you love."

–**Shanda Sumpter**, entrepreneur and founder, Heartcore Business, author, Core Calling.
www.heartcorebusiness.com - San Diego, CA.

"Judith has the innate ability to take you on an experiential journey inward. By dissecting your personal story, Judith guides you to see yourself as an unlimited possibility and as the courageous author of all that is to come. Through her teachings, readers will experience an awakening that leads them to knowing themselves deeply and profoundly. Judith's work is far beyond motivation, it's an invitation to all participants to be transformed. As this book expands the reach of her message throughout the world, I highly encourage everyone to absorb every word.

I was personally exposed to Judith's work 40 years ago and privileged to witness her evolution into the foremost master facilitator and coach. She can definitely rock your world having you shift perspective and experience all that you think you know from a different point of view. People say you can't change the past, but through my personal association with Judith I know you can. You just have to look at it differently."

–**Chuck Leibold**, President, LaPaz Mortgage
www.lapazmortgage.com- Laguna Hills, CA.

"I had the honor to staff an event led by Dr. Judith Rich. The experience changed my life. I would form one of the most loving and invaluable relationships of my life with Dr. Rich. Her teachings have been a catalyst for my development, continually stretching me beyond my limits, thus enabling me to be in the greatest possible service to those around me.

I am so grateful that the teachings of her life's work are now available in this book. May it serve as a map to unlock the highest potential of everyone who reads it and perpetuate the rise of consciousness throughout the world."

–**Gabriel J. Messuti**, Owner / Founder SUMMUS BODY |
MIND www.summusbodymind.com - Morristown, New Jersey

Acknowledgments

Mira Grace Pelham, this book is for you. Your arrival into this world five years ago at 24 weeks into my daughter's pregnancy, and weighing 1.8 pounds was nothing short of a miracle. Your name announces who you are, a Miracle and a Grace. You are the promise of the future. You inspire me to keep going. May your journey be as blessed as you have blessed mine.

Your team of Earthly angels will always have your back. This book is for them too. Chief among the Earthly Angels is Mira's mother, Gina Mazza, and her Auntie, Mia Mazza, my beloved daughters. I'm so proud of the beautiful, powerful and capable women you've become. You are courageous, kind, generous, resilient and loving. I dedicate this book to you with deep gratitude for your steadfast love and support of me through many chapters of rough and smooth waters.

I can't imagine going through life never having known, loved and been loved by these amazing people and my dearest friends Cara Barker, Eleanor Hanauer, and Lise Miller. You have left an imprint on my heart and soul and brought infinite goodness to my life. Your names are etched in my heart forever.

To the healers, teachers, and mentors who brought me to the deeper waters –Francoise Bourzat, Andriette Earl, Deb and Darryl Hobson, James Moore, Randy Revel –you opened my eyes to a deeper wisdom I never knew was in me.

To the thousands of people all over the world with whom I've had the privilege of working both as fellow trainers, students, interpreters and company owners, over the past four decades, this book is for you. To my friends and students in Mexico and Russia, in Taiwan and China, this book is for you. To Erik Esparza and Gabriel Messuti, your journeys in this work are just beginning. Keep on inspiring people and waking them up to their own greatness. To Shanda Sumpter, this book is for you. Keep playing big, creating your dreams and building platforms for others to live their own big lives.

Because of all of you, I am inspired to press forward, stand up, speak up and share my truth. Because of you, I'm still young at heart and passionate about my own brave new life ahead. I offer my deepest gratitude to all of you for touching my soul and leaving your mark on my heart. You all inspired me to bring this book into the world. And I'm forever grateful.

Table of Contents

Introduction

This is a book about finding the courage to change your life when you're torn between the need to cling to what is known and predictable, and being compelled by an inner urge to grow beyond what you already know. At the point where those two conflicting needs meet, there is a gap. This book is about getting inside that gap, finding the tools to re-invent yourself, build your courage, and create a brave new life beyond the box.

Inside your comfort zone, you know the game. You've carefully set up your life to be predictable with no surprises. You've screened and filtered out the people and events that could potentially shake things up. And because comfort zones are designed for, guess what, comfort, you can remain in your nice little nest, pull up the covers and settle in for a stress free life. And sooner or later, like Rip Van Winkle, you'll fall asleep.

And then one day, you wake up and realize that stress free life feels more like a prison than a cozy nest. What used to have you feel safe and secure, now feels like a suit of armor, encasing your entire body. You yearn to break free and break loose. You long to know what lies beyond that box, constructed so long ago from your limiting beliefs, fears, unexpressed emotions, painful memories, and stories from your past. You long to grow and explore the territory beyond what you already know. And finally, one day, you build up the courage to lean out, break free and rise up.

This book is about what it takes to make the journey from inside the box to beyond the box. It seems like such a short distance. How could it be so difficult to take that step? How is it you've spent your entire life in resistance to making this leap? How much of your energy have you invested in keeping the walls of the box intact? How many wondrous possibilities have you missed, having chosen instead to remain inside what you felt you could control?

These are the myths you'll be confronting as we journey together beyond the box. I have taken this journey with thousands of people during the past forty-three years in my career as a personal and leadership development trainer.

For decades, I have coached clients and trained participants in countries all over the world to "think outside the box". I have taught them that in order to create different results than the ones we currently have, we must think differently and take different kinds of actions than the ones we've always taken. That is still sound advice. But it's no longer enough simply to think outside the box.

In today's environment, change is happening so quickly we often don't even have time to consider "thinking" outside the box. Why? Because we have entered a time where whatever box inside which we might have thought we were thinking has been blown to smithereens and is nothing more than a memory. The very idea of having a comfort zone is becoming history. Change is now happening so rapidly, we must learn to adapt our ideas about what constitutes comfort. We are evolving into a new species of humans who no longer have comfort as an option. In other words, we must learn to become comfortable being uncomfortable!

In case you're still holding on to the shreds of that old box, still hoping there's light at the end of that tunnel, still wanting to play safe and thinking that strategy will produce the satisfying life you yearn to live, I hate to tell you, but that ship has sailed. The old box has been shredded and is on its way to recycling.

So what's the alternative? What comes after the box is gone? Aren't peace and comfort what everyone wants? Isn't that what we all work so hard to achieve? Why should anyone give up a life of comfort and choose instead to confront their fear? Why would I, or anyone, suggest that a more creative, fulfilling life lies beyond the box? What constitutes an "uncomfortable life" that is actually worth living? I've written this book to address these questions as they lie at the heart of what drives 99% of human behavior.

For starters, how about learning to live from a fuller expression of your potential, with freedom, courage, choice and creativity as your guideposts? How about welcoming the opportunity to create a life that is not based on old beliefs, patterns, attitudes and opinions? Why not embrace the idea that you can learn to operate free of the expectations of parents, teachers and other well-meaning people who planted their own fears into what became your "box" where you took up the mantle and lived as if it were your own? Let's learn to live bravely. Let's learn to lean out, break free and rise up to the challenges that face us as human beings on the planet in the twenty-first century.

If you're facing these questions in your own life, this book is for you. Think of this as the manual for upgrading your life when the old manual has become outdated. It offers practical advice on how to develop the necessary skills needed to prepare you for living that brave, new life you desire.

Each chapter addresses issues we're all facing as we face these turbulent times and offers guidance for how to find your way towards living a purposeful and satisfying life beyond the box.

My intention is to have this book support you to update the files on your mental, emotional and spiritual hard drives. Which files need deleting because their programming has kept you stuck? What new files are necessary to help you move forward and create the life you want now?

Our job, as human beings inhabiting planet Earth today, is to develop the inner and outer skills necessary to find ourselves again and again as we get caught in the riptides of change and lose our way. Life today dictates you learn these skills and do this work.

In spite of the chaos, disruption and turbulence, we can learn to not only survive but also thrive in these times. We can use this time as an opportunity to clean our inner house, take a reckoning of ourselves, discover who we are, and learn to build courage and resilience. We can learn to use the energy of chaos and turbulence to create lasting, transformational change in our lives, if we're willing to prepare ourselves and participate fully.

One thing is for certain: we're not going back from whence we came. But neither do we know what lies ahead. We only know we have within ourselves the raw material from which to forge a creative and satisfying life, even in the face of unprecedented change, and even if we don't yet know how to access that raw material. We can sense its potential and that's the fuel we're going to use to build out that brave, new life.

Are you ready to begin? So am I. Let's get started.

CHAPTER ONE

Change: An Orientation

I n the past year, parts of the U.S. and Caribbean Islands were decimated by a series of category 4 and 5 hurricanes, leaving behind massive destruction and a humanitarian crisis. In these natural disasters, millions of people lost their homes, many lost their lives, and parts of Puerto Rico are still without power or clean water months after the initial impact of the storms.

Whether or not you've been directly impacted by one of these events, to be alive today feels like living inside a hurricane. We might spend time in the eye where life appears to be calm and then quickly be thrown off course into the turbulent outer bands of the storm, tossed about by the velocity of the winds of change taking place in the world today.

In the U.S., we have entered a period of political upheaval with a new administration and a new president who is unlike anyone we've ever seen in that office. It appears that all the old ways of government which people have come to think of as "normal" have been turned on their heads. There is a new normal in town, but it is changing so quickly, it's difficult to even explain or define what it is. It seems we are in a time when the very idea of normal no longer applies. Change is happening so quickly, nothing has a chance to become the norm, except the very idea of change itself.

While change may be the new normal, there is nothing new about the idea of change. It's always been with us. What is new is the velocity and scale at which it's happening. These category 4 and 5 hurricanes are perfect metaphors for the kind of change and disruption we are witnessing in the world today.

Even the word "disruption" has gone mainstream in our thinking and speaking. No longer is the idea of disruption something we think of as an outlier. Companies like Uber, Airbnb, and Facebook have created massive ripples in their industries and completely changed the way consumers do business.

We are leaving traditional practices behind and are heading into a "brave new world" where the rules are being written and re-written on the fly. The proverbial "box" has already exploded and we are left with the task of picking up the pieces, and reinventing ourselves in a new way, equipped to meet that brave new world with gusto and courage.

Change is not a tidy process. Anyone who's ever been through a divorce, quit or lost their job knows that endings are often messy and starting over can be even more difficult. Or as Marilyn Ferguson, author of *The Aquarian Conspiracy* put it:

"It's not so much that we're afraid of change or so in love with the old ways, but it's that place in between that we fear … It's like being between trapezes. It's Linus when his blanket is in the dryer. There's nothing to hold on to."

When you are deep in a cycle of change and feel lost, like Linus, take heart. We're all in this together … When you feel like a trapeze artist swinging high above the circus floor of your life and you've just let go of your past but your future has not yet arrived, take heart. You're not alone. When you're in that place in between trapezes, in free fall and you can't even see if there's another trapeze coming your way, guess what? You're not all by yourself.

Imagine jumping out of an airplane and you have no parachute. All you have is a piece of fabric, a needle and a spool of thread. Your task is to make a parachute while you're falling, finish it and have it open before you hit the ground. Sound daunting? When you're going through disruptive change your life can feel like that.

For others it can feel like walking through quicksand. The trick is to know where to place your foot and how fast to move. You could step into the abyss and disappear, or you could place your feet on solid ground and live to take another step. Each one could lead to either triumph or tragedy.

Change doesn't come with an instruction manual. When change is afoot, all bets are off. We can work hard, plan and prepare and then Life happens. We either end up where we wanted to go or we end up somewhere else.

The steepness of the learning curve in a cycle of rapid change is like being in a master class in learning how to dance on a tightrope in high heels going backwards. Missteps are likely. Mistakes made early in the learning curve equip you to navigate the steeper terrain later on, *provided* you learn from them. The keyword here is *learn*. Mistakes are a most potent teacher!

> *"I've missed more than 9,000 shots in my career. I've lost almost 300 games. Twenty-six times I've been trusted to take the game winning shot and missed. I've failed over and over again in my life and that is why I succeed."*

Michael Jordan

So don't be afraid to fail. If you haven't had at least one failure under your belt, it means you've played too small, stayed too comfortable and never dared to color outside the lines. Now's a great time to begin! We're out here searching for new ways to navigate this slippery terrain together.

> *"Our finest moments are most likely to occur when we are*
> *feeling deeply uncomfortable, unhappy, or unfulfilled.*
> *For it is only in such moments, propelled by our discomfort,*
> *that we are likely to step out of our ruts and start*
> *searching for different ways or truer answers."*

M. Scott Peck

No matter the external circumstances, every human being comes to a point when the path they're on takes a sudden turn, comes to a fork in the road or dead ends. When confronted with unexpected, unpredictable and unwanted change, what do you do? Where do you turn? How do you choose the best course to chart and get yourself turned in a direction that moves your life forward? This book is intended to help you chart that course.

For many, the path ahead is obscured by fear, depression, intense emotions, conflicting advice from others, a history of failure, self-limiting beliefs and past conditioning that has them convinced they'll never find their way. Others don't see their way because they haven't identified the path they want to travel, so how can they be sure if they're on it or not? This book is an operator's manual for learning how to work with and move past fear and self-limiting beliefs.

Even as I write this book, the norms around change are no longer the norms and a new chapter of how to effect change is unfolding right before our eyes. Today a brave, new consciousness is emerging in our young people, the *post-Millennial* generation sometimes called *Gen Z*. Born out of their frustration at the unwillingness and inability of adults, our current leaders on the state and national levels, to tackle the gun safety issue, high school students are becoming the new generation of activists in the U.S. and around the world. They are leading the way to push state legislatures to enact sane gun legislation and they demonstrate a greater willingness to embrace diversity in sexual orientation, immigration, and race. They are writing a new chapter around issues that have polarized and paralyzed American society for decades.

These young people are showing adults what change looks like and how it works in the twenty-first century. I hope I live long enough to see this generation take its place as the leaders of our country. They are the living, breathing demonstration of what we (in the world of transformation) have been teaching for over forty years. These are the Jonathan Livingston Seagulls, come to teach the rest of us how to fly. They will not be bound by what the older seagulls (the rest of us) think is possible. They know that to reach their potential they must break through thousands of years of hardened beliefs that have kept the flock flying low and close to the shore, fighting each other for scraps, in fear and struggling to survive.

They are the drift-busters, the mind-shifters, the change-makers, the paradigm-breakers. They have come to teach a new way to live together on a shrinking planet with dwindling resources.

They are moving the ball down the field, unstoppable in their dedication and passion to take the lead and show the way forward. They are not afraid to confront the established ways and norms of how adults have resisted change. Quite the opposite! Today's generation of young adults, some as young as 14 years old, having been the target of mass shootings in the places that were always considered safe sanctuaries, places like schools and churches, are no longer waiting for adults to take the lead. They are pushing their way to the forefront of changing the minds and hearts of those in charge and they are making progress.

They are demonstrating that the key is not to be tied to the way things have always been, but to marry their anger and frustration with their passion and dedication to move ahead and set a higher bar for what is possible. They are exploding the box of societal and political norms and re-inventing the game of how to effect change. My money is on them.

For older people, change on this scale is anything but comfortable. Old beliefs, patterns, attitudes and behaviors are being called into question and new norms are replacing them at a rapid pace. The opportunity for all of us now is to learn to adapt quickly and get comfortable being uncomfortable. Many people will learn to thrive in the difficult times ahead. Why not you? I've written this book to support you in your own process of navigating change, however it's manifesting in your life right now.

Food for Thought

- What are the most challenging changes you are facing today? Personal relationships? Career? Health? Finances? All of the above?

- What is holding you back from being decisive and taking action in these areas?

- If you weren't afraid to fail, what steps would you take today to get unstuck?

CHAPTER TWO

We're Not in Kansas Anymore

Much of the time, like a hurricane, change visits our lives uninvited. But what about when you know that you want and need to make significant changes in your life but you're stuck in old patterns or paralyzed by fear? How do you get unstuck and get started in a new direction? How do you overcome your resistance to taking on what appears to be impossible, too scary, or beyond your ability? Feel free to add any of your own excuses for why you haven't already broken free. You have an entire library of them. More on that in a later chapter.

Like many people, I spent most of my early years in life going along with the program laid out for me by teachers, friends, employers and others who influenced me. I wanted to belong, fit in, be accepted, and be popular among my peers. But most of all I wanted to live up to my parents' expectations and become the person I thought they wanted me to be.

My mother, born in 1910, and one of ten children, married my father at age 17. Hers was another mouth to feed in this large family, so she was encouraged to find a man, get married, and be one less responsibility for her parents. In fact, when she was eight years old, my grandparents literally gave her away to go live with her aunt, the sister of my grandmother. Aunt Alice was childless. My grandma Nellie had ten children. Why not share a little bit of the excess? It sounded like a good plan to the adults.

The day Aunt Alice came to choose which child she wanted, she chose my mother because she had bright red, wavy hair and stood out from all the others. Aunt Alice took my mother by the hand and led her out of the only home she'd ever known, and to her own house to live and to become her child. The only problem was no one had ever mentioned this arrangement to my mom. In her eight-year old mind, her parents had abandoned her. And why wouldn't she think that? That is basically what happened.

As my mom tells the story, she cried nonstop for three weeks. Imagine being one of ten children, with all of her siblings as close family members, to being an only child, living with people who weren't exactly total strangers, but they might as well have been.

Talk about change? Talk about disruption? Except my mother refused to get on board. She cried until Aunt Alice gave up and returned her home to her own parents and family. But even as she went back home, my mom was dramatically altered. She definitely wasn't in Kansas anymore!

She no longer felt secure in her family, and saw her position among them as very fragile. Her parents might decide to get rid of her in some other way, thought this little eight-year old girl. She decided she'd better earn the right to stay put.

From that time on, she took it upon herself to become indispensable in her family. She became the one who took care of the others. At the end of the school day, she lagged behind and made sure everyone got home from school intact. She made sure her brothers and sisters were safe and secure, no doubt a compensation for her lack of these feelings in herself.

As she grew older, it was clear to her that her path to security lay in getting married and being able to move out on her own. Is it any wonder that the main message I got from her as a girl and then a young woman growing up was: "You need a man in your life to take care of you."

I got that message loud and clear and never questioned its veracity for myself. And so, my own life unfolded as a fulfillment of my mother's message, for I took it as a warning. I became a woman who thought she needed a man to take care of her. I became a woman who couldn't see who she was or what she was capable of on her own. For I was convinced that my mother was right and that I needed a man to take care of me. It would take several decades and three divorces for me to sort it all out and become a woman capable of managing her own life.

Born in 1942, I was raised to believe that my primary job was to graduate from high school, get married, work for a while and then have a family. A "career" was only "something to fall back on" after the children grew up or in the case of extreme necessity. Women were not expected in those days to have legitimate careers of their own, outside of their roles as wife and mother. Of course, there were always the exceptions. Some women did go into professional careers as doctors or lawyers, but they were a distinct minority. Most careers open to women were the good "fall back on" kinds of careers: teaching, nursing, or some kind of secretarial work.

I entered high school in 1956, and had to decide if I was going to take the college prep track or the vocational track. Because no one in my family had gone to college, there were no expectations for me to go. My father naturally thought I would become a secretary, no college degree necessary. The skills needed were typing, filing, operating a telephone, taking dictation, and some organizational skills.

I was fourteen years old. I could look ahead and see my future if I chose the path my parents expected me to take. My older brother had just gotten married to his childhood sweetheart, who was an "executive secretary". She was a beautiful woman, inside and out, who wore her own self-designed, exquisitely handmade, clothes to work every day and was the epitome of the *Mad Men* type of secretary. She was refined, soft-spoken and charming. At 6 ft. tall, she was willowy, like a model, and had the looks to match. Years later, she and my brother divorced (another first in the family) and she actually did become a runway model, working for the big fashion houses in Paris and throughout Europe.

But as for me at age 14, I peered into that future (called "secretary) and knew it was not for me. This was the very first time in my life when I took a peek beyond what had always been my box. It was the very first time I even considered that I needed to make my own choice, independent of what my parents wanted for me. They wanted me to choose the tried and true path of doing office work. This was the safe choice because this was what they knew. It was the choice to stay in Kansas (metaphorically speaking).

But it wasn't what was written on my heart. I wanted to be a teacher and that meant going to college and getting a degree in education. And that meant choosing the college track in high school. And so I did. To their credit, my parents were in full support of my choice. I studied liberal arts in high school, and went on to college. I loved the school environment and my chosen major so much, I attended summer school every year and earned enough credits to graduate a semester early. I couldn't wait to get started in my first teaching job!

However, even as I chose my own path in terms of education and becoming a teacher, my early conditioning was still imprinted very strong in me. I was still the woman who believed she needed a man to take care of her. The week after I graduated from college with a fresh teaching degree in my hand and a job teaching special education, I married my college sweetheart. I didn't need a career to fall back on; I needed a husband to fall back on!

Or so I thought. And yet, my soul knew this was not my truth. I knew walking down the aisle in my first marriage I had made a mistake. I knew I didn't want to be married, but I didn't have the courage to turn around and leave the church. That's what my heart and soul wanted me to do. But I couldn't disappoint my parents, my future husband, and all the relatives who had come to witness our vows.

I went through the motions that day, knowing all the while that my heart wasn't in it, hoping that I would grow to love this man, grow to love being a wife, grow to accept these new roles. It was a lose/lose proposition from the start, and you can guess how it unfolded. Within two years, we were divorced. But my mother's warning "you need a man in your life" would continue to haunt me and I allowed it to undermine my ability to hear and know my own truth.

It would take me three marriages and three divorces to figure out that "needing a man to take care of me" and being a traditional wife was not my truth. It was not what was written on my heart. I kept trying to fit myself back into the old box. I had the education, I had the career, I had the marriage, and a second marriage that would include two children. But something was not right with my soul. I felt like I was living someone else's life. Not my own. However, I didn't know what my own life was supposed to look like. I loved my children, I loved being a mother, but my soul was restless. I was not at home with myself. Something had to change.

I yearned to know who I was and what my soul wanted for my life. I'd been on automatic for the first three decades of my life. Even though I'd chosen to go to college and become something other than a secretary (no offense to secretaries!), I was pulled back into the old box of "wife, mother, stay-at-home-mom".

The more restless I became in those roles, the more my marriages began to falter. I was not conscious enough at that time to understand that the change that wanted to happen in me had nothing to do with a marriage or a husband. It was about me wanting to know, love and accept myself. But I didn't know that, at least consciously.

Do I have regrets about those marriages and divorces? Yes and no. Looking back, with the advantage of hindsight and greater perspective, I can see how I could have done things differently. But I didn't have that wisdom or perspective at the time. I made choices back then that got me into marriage out of fear and insecurity and had me stay out of fear and insecurity, leave out of restlessness and dissatisfaction, then jump back into another marriage out of fear and insecurity! Was I being the most empowered version of myself? Was I making choices that were aligned with my soul and its purpose? I never even considered these questions. I was too driven by fear.

The no regrets part is that I see, with the advantage of hindsight, as former U.N General Secretary Dag Hammarskjold said: *"How long the road is. But for all the time the journey has already taken, how you have needed every second of it in order to learn what the road passes by."*

I needed every second of the journey I've taken to learn the lessons I was required to learn. And so I see that while it was painful, it was also purposeful. And that's how the soul works. More on that in a later chapter.

And then one day my whole life changed. Encouraged by a friend, I attended a personal development seminar. It was my first exposure to the human potential movement, the first time I looked inside at myself and the experience changed my life. My journey of transformation had begun.

Changing my life was exactly why I went in the first place. Having lived my life up until then as someone who didn't know who she was or what she wanted, all I knew was that I felt restless, and yearned for something more than the life I'd been living. Something deep inside was stirring in me and calling me forth. I was afraid to know what it meant, because if I allowed myself to know, I'd be forced to do something about it that I feared would cause pain for my family. If I really took action on what was stirring in me, I couldn't bear to face the amount of disappointment I would cause to my loved ones.

From the outside, my life appeared to be perfect. However, inside, I felt lost and disconnected. I was not at home in or with myself and had no idea how to find that elusive place called home for which I yearned. I had followed my mother's instructions about having a man in my life to take care of me, in spite of the fact that something in me knew this wasn't true. It wasn't *my* truth, but rather the truth my mother had accepted for herself. A greater truth awaited my discovery. I was both scared and excited to find out what it was.

"The Wiz" was a popular Broadway musical back in 1975 and every time I heard the song "Home", I broke into tears. It spoke to a longing in me I couldn't name or put words to.

> *Maybe there's a chance for me to go back*
> *Now that I have some direction*
> *It would sure be nice to go back home*
> *Where there's love and affection*
> *And just maybe I can convince time to slow up*
> *Giving me enough time in my life to grow up*
> *Time be my friend, Let me start again.*

I knew the *home* in these lyrics didn't refer to a physical place. Wherever it was, I couldn't find it in myself and I didn't know where to look for it elsewhere. My marriage was faltering, and I felt in my heart I needed to leave it in order to find myself. Yet I couldn't find the courage to take the first step in breaking free and charting a course to my own life. The stakes were high: two daughters, a husband who loved me. Who would want to leave such a life? I knew it sounded crazy and I was afraid to hear or know my own truth, that in spite of everything, I needed to go.

My experience in that training room turned my life upside down. Everything in me that had been locked down, buttoned up, and super-glued in place came undone. I had literally exploded my box, broke free and rose up. It was both terrifying and liberating.

Change is like that: terrifying and liberating. The terrifying part is what keeps most people from ever dipping their toes in its water. It's also what keeps us stuck. Today, I know that my experience of exploding my own box back in 1975 is exactly what my soul ordered so that I could start to excavate myself from the rubble of my life. It took years to sort through all the pieces and put them back together in a way that reflected, not who I'd been taught or conditioned to be, but who I really was.

The woman who emerged from the pieces shocked and surprised me. Like Dorothy in the *Wizard of Oz*, she wasn't in Kansas anymore. She was far more courageous that I'd ever dreamed of being. She was strong and brave and unafraid to take a stand for what she believed in. She was passionate about people and wanting others to have the same opportunity to wake up and discover themselves as she had. When she finally shook off her slumber, she realized she was here with a distinct purpose and a mission to fulfill. It wasn't enough for her to wake up and live an empowered life. She realized it's what everyone has come to the planet to do. Writing this book is part of fulfilling that mission.

She's the woman I've become. In my life I've been a teacher, therapist, coach, trainer, speaker and writer. I've led seminars for thousands of individuals and numerous organizations in the U.S., Russia, Asia, Mexico and several other countries in Latin America.

In addition, I'm the mother of two mighty women and the grandmother of a wondrous little girl, Mira Grace, who keeps me on my toes and challenges me to keep up with her. She and my daughters are my constant inspiration and motivation to keep going and keep doing what I'm doing, now, in what would normally be a time in my life when I might expect to retire.

Retire? That feels like Kansas to me. I can't imagine it. There's too much work left to do, not only in my personal life, but also on the planet. There are still so many people who are in search of themselves and their rightful path in this lifetime. I'm not ready to hang it up just yet. Especially now, when the plot for humanity continues to thicken and the stakes for our collective survival keep getting higher. In many respects, at age 76, I feel like I'm just getting started. Perhaps that's what keeps me feeling young and energized. I have work to do! And so do you. Let's get busy!

Food for Thought

- Go back into your personal story and see if you can find the time when you first became aware of the need for change in your life.

- What was not working in your life the way you wanted it to work?

- What was your initial response to the call for change?

- What kept you stuck or in resistance? What were you afraid of?

- What fears do you still carry today around this subject?

- What are you currently waiting for before you feel you can take concrete action to make these changes?

- How much longer do you need to stay where you are?

CHAPTER THREE

Learning to Surf the Rough Waters of Change

Many people find themselves uprooted later in life when a loved one dies or a long-term relationship or marriage ends. When all the props of your life are pulled out from under you, where do you find solid ground? If you've always identified yourself by the work you do or where you live or the size of your bank balance and those things are ripped away, who are you now?

Consider the story of Tim, a man in his mid-fifties. He was married to the same woman for 28 years, the father of two grown daughters, and owned and ran his own successful small business for 20 years. To anyone looking on the outside, his life was the picture of stability. And then, seemingly in the flash of an eye, everything changed.

Years of discontent that had been buried came to the surface when he discovered that his wife had been having a secret affair for several years. Somehow he had managed to miss or avoid seeing the clues, a testament to his own level of detachment from the emotional needs of his wife were now being met by someone else.

Talk about a wake-up call! His life turned upside down in an instant. He'd discovered that nothing was as it appeared to be. In his haste to bury his feelings of loss and betrayal, on the rebound, he soon began a relationship with another woman. He and his wife eventually separated and got divorced. A couple of years later, he married the woman he turned to in his despair. Can you sense where this going?

Shortly into this second marriage, he discovered his new wife engaging in inappropriate behavior with men on the Internet. Devastated, he tried very hard through couples therapy to work out whatever issues were driving her behavior. Obviously, there were two sides to the story, but ultimately, after three years of a marriage characterized by constant turmoil, they decided to divorce. At the very same time, Tim decided to sell his business and move on. He was now deep in the change cycle. His entire life was being transformed. Now in his late 50s Tim discovered it was time for him to reinvent himself from the inside out, top to bottom. And he did.

Tim wiped the slate of everything his old life had embodied. Having left a second marriage and sold his business, he was now completely untethered to everything that had anchored his identity and defined who he thought he was.

Do you think this was comfortable or easy? Absolutely not! But it seemed as though his life was driving him into new territory. He could either choose to resist and fight this change wanting to happen or he could surrender, accept and go with the flow. He chose the latter. And not without paying some significant prices emotionally, financially, spiritually and physically.

In the face of such massive change, and with a lot of support from friends and his own intense desire to grow Tim saw the opportunity to reframe who he was and how he saw himself interacting in the world.

He was willing to do the inner work necessary to align himself with his new identity and role.

Today, ten years after the change cycle first began, he has started and sold another business, is now retired and engaged to be married to a woman he met on the other side of his healing process. He is in no hurry to marry this time. He and his fiancée, who is a few years older than he and also retired, enjoy a life of travel, fun and friendship together, spending several weeks each year traveling to places on their bucket lists, sharing the fun of cooking and entertaining friends. With his oldest daughter now married, Tim is looking forward to the day when he gets to become a grandfather for the first time.

It has been a challenging decade for Tim. A hurricane of change disrupted his life, exploded his box and blew him to smithereens. And today, he would tell you he has never been happier or felt more grounded in his entire life.

Tim's story might sound scary to a lot of readers. Too much change, too quickly! Too much feeling of being out of control! How can anyone manage to survive such turbulence? How can one lose everything and not be destroyed in the process? If the voices in your head are telling you you're worthless because you no longer have "Job, House, Marriage or Bank Account Charming" how do you learn to not only survive, but also transform the chaos into an opportunity to grow and thrive?

> *"It is not the strongest of the species that survives, nor the most intelligent, but the ones most responsive to change."*

Charles Darwin

Human beings are hard wired to seek certainty and limit their exposure to the unpredictable. We want to have "everything under control". To a degree, having everything under control is desirable and to a lesser degree, somewhat possible. It depends on how we define "everything".

If what we mean by "everything" lies within our 2% sphere of control, the chances increase that we'll be successful. But consider the other 98%! How do we handle life when most of it is out of our control?

Inside the old box, life is designed to be predictable and settled. No surprises are welcome here. However, we can see how quickly it all can change and the idea of being in control goes out the window. If you are attached to being in control of everything, or at least thinking you are, then a change cycle is going to be difficult. It will demand that you let go and allow what is coming to come. You can fight it, but to do so will cost you mightily.

Don't waste time trying to control the uncontrollable. Change happens. It doesn't care if you agree and want it. Change doesn't wait for you to be ready. So what *can* you do?

Where to begin?

I suggest you learn to surf in the rough waters created when life invited you or you were pushed to break free of your box and head into new territory. These conditions require you to stretch yourself and kick up your courage a few notches. If this sounds intimidating and you tell yourself "this is not for me", consider this: you're in it already! You'll either learn how to surf or you'll sink. Which do you choose?

Today's environment demands that we rewire ourselves and adopt a new model for how we respond to life, one that allows us to replace the old, automatic reactions with the ability to choose how we frame what happens in each moment. This is a learnable skill. Remember the story of Tim and how he reinvented himself from the inside out? If he could do it, so can you.

What is required is a conscious intention, practice, and an ally, someone who will interrupt your old patterns when they rear their ugly heads. If you've always been a Lone Ranger, now would be the time to seek out an ally. This could be a trusted friend, a therapist, a coach, or a member of the clergy. Or join a mastermind group. Who can you trust to have your back and tell you the inconvenient truth when it needs telling?

If you want to master surfing the rough waters of change, you'd better also transform your relationship with fear, for if not, fear will win every time. Isn't that what's kept you in the prison of your box in the first place? You gave your power to the voices of fear inside your head and have allowed your fear to be in charge. Isn't it time to make friends with your fear? Really? Make friends? Yes. Let's look.

Making Friends With Fear

Faced with circumstances over which we have no control, we become fearful and powerless. When these feelings get stuck in the body, they're like gigantic pools of toxic stress. When stopped in our tracks and we don't know what to do, our stomach gets tied in knots. We lose sleep, get irritable and often take out our fear and frustration on innocent others. What if you could make friends with your fear instead?

Surfing in rough waters can be scary and requires that we learn how to have a healthy relationship with fear because fear is going to be our constant companion. If you think the way to manage fear is to push it away, ignore, deny or avoid it, you'll be in for an even rougher ride. There is another way to be with fear. It requires that we make friends with it. Cozy up to it. Sound daunting? It is! But that's the very point.

Remember Dorothy in the *Wizard of Oz* and her adventures on the Yellow Brick Road? On her way to meet the Wizard and find out how to get back home, she met a cast of characters, all in search of something they thought they were lacking. The Tin Man was in search of a heart, for he was unable to feel. The Scarecrow was in search of a brain, for he thought himself lacking in the ability to reason and learn. The Cowardly Lion was in search of his courage, for he was not brave like a lion should be. And dear Dorothy felt lost and disoriented, blown by a tornado far from home. All she wanted to do was to find her way back home.

We all know how this story goes. When they finally found the Wizard, he sent them on a task that required they confront their greatest fears, find the Wicked Witch of the West, slay her, and take back the ruby red slippers. This story of course, is also the story of the hero's journey. It's the story of us. It's the story of the journey we all must take to confront the dragons in our lives and take back our power.

One way to think about fear is:

False

Evidence

Appearing

Real

To the subconscious mind, fear isn't just a feeling or a thought. Fearful thoughts get blown up and projected onto the screen of the subconscious mind and end up appearing as WILD UNTAMED BEASTS! They appear to be real with the ability to threaten your existence. And they can, IF you grant them that power. So let's look at how to deal with fear in an empowering way.

Strategies for Dealing with Fear
Befriend it

I picture fear as a little gerbil. You know, the cute, little furry animal that runs around on a wheel. This image levels the playing field and puts things in a more helpful perspective. It allows you to bring fear back down to size so you can sit with, embrace, and defang it. Once you realize the fear as energy instead of being a "thing", you'll become aware of more options for how to be with that energy, how to use it to be creative. Fear can be an ally if you know how to work with it in a conscious way.

Get quiet – discover your inner oasis

When life becomes chaotic and the gerbil is racing around the wheel, tap yourself on the shoulder and tell yourself to "stop". Stop the mind chatter and knee-jerk reactions. Gently pluck the gerbil off the wheel. With loving kindness, sit down together in a rocking chair and cuddle up with a cup of warm tea and a nice blanket. More than anything, the gerbil is the frightened part of you that wants to be loved. It also needs some R&R. Imagine how tired YOU'D be if you were running in circles all the time! Oh, you already are? Then pay close attention.

Close your eyes and pay attention to your breath. Take a few slow, easy breaths, following the inhalation and exhalation. Become aware of the spacious openness that holds and surrounds you and your breath. You and the gerbil, take a bath in this. Keep breathing into that spaciousness and stay here as long as you like. Even 5 minutes off the wheel will help to reset and refocus your mind. The world will still be there when you decide to return. A practice of stopping and resting in the breath is an important step that helps you reconnect to your own rhythm when the rhythm of the world overwhelms you. Invest fifteen to thirty minutes a day in your inner oasis and you'll reap enormous benefits.

Become aware of your experience

When you decide to return to the outer world, notice the ease you've just experienced. Before you resume activity, look to see what arises out of this openness. The world may be going to hell in a hand basket, but in this present moment, you have everything you'll ever need. Most of all, you have choice. You may not have choice about what is happening, but you always have choice about how to be with what's happening.

Consciously choose how to respond

Choose, not based on your conditioned history or your fears about the future. Choose based on *now*. Who knows, this could be your very last moment. If it were, what would you choose? Have the courage to choose that, now.

So you and the gerbil, take at least one 15-minute break each day and you'll both feel better. You'll then have the clarity of focus and energy to take action in the direction of what really matters in your life, like spending time loving the people you love and being a presence of peace in a stormy world.

Don't take it personally

Embrace the reality that life isn't happening to you; it's just happening. Most of what happens in life is not personal, although it may appear to be. When it rains, it's not raining on you; it's simply raining! If you walk in the world thinking that life is happening to you, you're destined to suffer. Life happens. And then you choose.

Be willing to give up old beliefs

You can start with your need to be right. The need to be right doesn't leave much space for learning outside what we already think or know. This is a hard one for most of us because our conditioning is so strong. We've been taught that to be anything other than right is akin to being a failure. It's not true. Don't believe everything you think. Sometimes we get frozen in fear, afraid to make a choice or take an action because we're afraid of being wrong or making a mistake.

Here's another way to approach the right/wrong paradigm: rather than viewing your current situation through the lens of is this right or wrong/good or bad, instead, look to see if this choice works or doesn't work. Does this choice empower you to take risks? Is your life moving ahead in a way that is rewarding and gives a sense of freedom? This is my definition of what works.

What perspectives and choices open new doors and forward your life, versus what choices paralyze you, cause you to recycle the same issues over and over, and prevent you from making progress? If you make choices that empower you to go forward instead, even though they're uncomfortable, you're on your way to getting unstuck and moving beyond your fear.

Get comfortable being uncomfortable

There's an ancient Chinese proverb used to heap curses upon an enemy: *"It's better to be a dog in a peaceful time than be a man in a chaotic period."* Some say its modern translation is *"May you live in interesting times."*

Who would argue that these times are not at the least "interesting"? The chaos of these times carries a significant degree of discomfort and requires that we learn to be comfortable being uncomfortable. If that sounds like a conundrum, it is. Remember, we humans are addicted to comfort and certainty. Being thrown off by rapid change often feels like being in "free fall". For most, free fall is not a natural or comfortable state. And yet, that's where we are.

The gift of these times is the demand that we wake up, stay awake and learn to be present in each moment. No falling asleep at the wheel or hitting the snooze button! Imagine the new opportunities waiting to be discovered in these dangerous times!

31

Food for Thought

- What change is happening or wanting to happen in your life right now?

- Where are you in the process? Beginning, middle, end?

- What signs do you see that orient you to where you are?

- What limiting beliefs do you need to give up to go forward?

- What would you do if you knew you couldn't fail?

CHAPTER FOUR

Starting Over vs. Reinventing Yourself

W hen I query people in personal development seminars about their purpose for attending, a majority of participants respond with:

I feel lost.
I don't have a direction for my life.
I lost my job, my marriage or my relationship. How do I start over?
I think I know where I want to go. I don't know how to get there.
I know what I don't want. I'm confused about what I do want.
I just graduated from college. How do I start my adult life?

Are you starting over or reinventing yourself?

Starting over is the process whereby we have come to an ending and eventually we begin something new or different. This process might not necessarily involve taking personal stock of our self, upgrading our skills or obtaining the psychological or emotional preparation necessary for what's next. It could simply mean ending a previous endeavor, be it a job or a relationship, and jumping into something new or different. We might be the same exact person we were in the previous endeavor. In this case, we could expect to create similar results in the new situation as we did the previous one. Nothing really changed except the landscape. The person doing the doing remained the same. This is not *always* the case when starting over, but it can often be a trap into which we fall. We think something has changed because we altered the exterior conditions. But if that exterior change is not accompanied by a change from within, by examining our limiting beliefs and behaviors, chances are we will re-create our old circumstances, but with a few new bells and whistles.

Reinventing oneself is a very different ball game. Reinvention is an inside job and requires that we literally create or invent ourselves anew from the inside out. We don't begin with our dissatisfaction or resistance to what came before. We're not changing out of reaction to something we don't like or don't want.

Reinvention begins with the questions: what is my vision and, based on my vision what do I want? The process of reinvention is driven by one's vision rather than by one's circumstances. Having a powerful vision to call you forth and guide you going forward is vital to support you in moving through fear and paralysis and building up courage and inspiration to navigate in rough waters.

When you've broken free of the box, and the winds of change and chaos prevail, feeling lost and uncertain of what to do next is a common experience. Beyond the box, we are tasked with figuring out how to even get started and begin our adult life or how to start over later in life.

Over a lifetime, most of us will reach a place where, in order to go forward, must let go of what no longer serves or works. Given the times in which we live, men and women of all ages can expect to reinvent themselves several times throughout their lives.

We can find ourselves thrown off course as part of a larger social or economic condition, as in a jobs crisis. A career one trained for may no longer hold the promise it once had. At other times we start over because we become disappointed or disillusioned in a career we thought was a perfect match and later discovered that reality didn't align with our expectations. Women who left careers to raise a family may find themselves back in the job market because of divorce or economic necessity.

Retirement age is another stage of development where reinvention becomes necessary. We used to think retirement meant sitting back, taking it easy, sleeping in late, and having the time to pursue those long lost dreams we left behind in the rat race of having to make a living.

For today's retirees, that scenario is likely a myth. Age discrimination is a major issue for people of retirement age who still need to work and face both dwindling financial resources and dwindling opportunities on the horizon.

Those who are fortunate enough to have adequate financial resources have the luxury of choosing when and if they want to stop working or change careers midstream. Many say they don't want to keep doing what they've been doing, but they don't know what to do next.

For those who have worked hard and saved enough money to retire and live comfortably, this can also be a crisis point. If all your eggs have been in the basket called "my job, my work, or my career", and that chapter is over, who are you now? If you've identified yourself as your job title, or by the work you do, and you're no longer doing that work, who are you now? How does one transform the energy that previously went into their work life into a satisfying personal life?

It's the Linus without a blanket syndrome. The challenge is to redirect the energy and passion and commitment that once went into the work life into finding a new source of expression in the world. What if starting over wasn't a chore but just a new adventure?

Elaine worked for thirty-five years in a field in which she was both inspired and inspirational. She gave herself 1000% to her work. It was her mission and purpose for being on the planet. And she was very accomplished in what she did. But as the years went by, she became aware that giving her 1000% was taking a toll on her health and body. Giving less than 1000% was not an option for her. It simply wasn't how she operated. Since she was unwilling to compromise how she did the work, she made the choice to retire. Her heart was still saying "yes", but her body was saying "no".

Because she'd always been prudent with money, Elaine was financially secure at this point in her life. Her house was paid for. She had money in the bank and money invested in safe and conservative investments. She was very comfortable in this area of her life. However, giving up her career was a difficult choice to make. Her entire identity had been wrapped up in her work. But in her soul, she knew it was time to go. Time to reinvent herself, start again and find a new way to contribute her passion and energy.

Elaine is still searching for a vehicle to express her desire to make a difference in the world. I sense that Elaine's soul is taking her on a journey to find the way forward. Faith and trust in herself and the process are her two main assignments now. These have always been her issues. My point again – we cannot escape the work the soul has come to do. One way or another, it will have its way with us. We can resist for a lifetime, but in the end, the soul always wins. And when it does, we win too.

Feeling lost and uncertain about what to do next is not limited to career issues. Relationships offer another domain of big challenges. People might find themselves stuck in a marriage that long ago lost its luster, yet are afraid or can't afford to leave; or they don't have the skills to make it better. And sometimes, career and relationship challenges clash and things get intense.

Susan came to me seeking coaching. She'd been in an abusive relationship for three years and didn't know how to end it. Every time she tried, her boyfriend put on the charm offensive to seduce her back into the relationship. And for a short while, things would get better. Her boyfriend treated her with the kindness and respect she wanted. But it didn't take long for things to go back to their default setting as the dynamic between them was set on "abuse". Susan felt he was capable of being a better person, so she hung on, hoping he would finally wake up and realize it for himself. She even played amateur therapist with him, rarely a good idea.

At the end of three years, after being in therapy and working with different healers and coaches, Susan still couldn't understand why she was unable to leave this abusive relationship. As we began to explore what lay beneath the surface in the realm of her subconscious beliefs, she discovered voices inside her that were the source of her own self-abuse. *"You'll never amount to anything; why should you even think you deserve to have someone love you? You're not loveable. Look at you! You're fat (she isn't). Who would want to be with you?"*

When Susan realized that she was the one who was abusing herself and that her boyfriend was merely echoing her own beliefs, the lights started to come on. She broke off the relationship and this time for good, within a week of our first coaching session.

While she's no longer in the abusive relationship with the boyfriend, Susan is now exploring those inner conversations that perpetuate the abuse, even though the boyfriend is no longer in the picture. The real abuser lives inside of her.

When we met, Susan was lost inside confusion about her inability to end the abuse. Now that she knows where the real abuse is coming from, the real work can begin.

What should you do when you're uncertain of what steps to take next? It's human nature to want predictability. We're creatures of habit who seek comfort and are not well equipped to handle the uncertainty that comes from finding ourselves at a dead end or in a cul-de-sac.

Few people have the skills to look beyond challenges that appear to obscure the path, or explore within to find the inner resources necessary to grow larger than those challenges. When faced with roadblocks that appear to be immovable, if we can't tap into our own resourcefulness, it's easy to get caught up in fear and anxiety, both of which make us feel lost and incapable of dealing with the crisis at hand.

Change sounds difficult and must require suffering. Right? It depends. It requires suffering *if* that's our belief. If we let fear choose for us, then we'll contract. To protect ourselves from what we think is painful, we armor ourselves and pull back from life as it's happening. We set ourselves up to suffer because that's the condition for which we've prepared. And guess what? We'll be right. We'll suffer. It's guaranteed.

Even under the most challenging of circumstances involving pain and hardship, suffering is not required. There is a Zen aphorism that says, *"Pain is inevitable; suffering is optional."*

Food for Thought

- What is most painful in your life right now?

- How long have you felt this way?

- What obstacles keep you from moving forward?

- How do you want this situation to be resolved?

- What is your vision for your life?

- What feels more challenging to you? Starting over or reinventing yourself? Which one will you do?

CHAPTER FIVE

The Soul and Change

I recall listening to John Denver's song *Sweet Surrender* in that life-changing seminar experience, and my heart cracked open. All the fear and uncertainty I'd held onto that kept me paralyzed and unable to recognize what I wanted for my life evaporated in those lyrics and I saw myself awake, alive and free, driving in a car with the top down and headed towards an uncertain future. It didn't matter that I didn't know where I was going. I was on my way. I knew that to find myself, I must go. And so I went into my own future, not knowing what lay ahead, but knowing I was being pulled by something more powerful than my fears. I would eventually come to know this "something" as the call of my soul.

Soul Process

The last forty years of my own journey have taken me into the territory of soul process, learning how to decipher and work with the soul. The late scholar and psychiatrist, James Hillman, has written extensively about the soul and its "code", a kind of imprint it must fulfill. According to Hillman, the soul has no preference how we unfold its agenda, only that we do. The soul will have its way with us, meaning it will steer our lives in the direction needed to meet the learning we are here to gain. If we're lost, stuck, abandoned, betrayed, abused, alone and confused, it's part of the soul's attempts to get our attention.

We might strike out on a certain path and travel it for eons and if we lose our way, we'll eventually end up in the desert, one of the soul's favorite places for doing its fine-tuning.

The soul is at home in the desert. Soul work is best done in the deep, quiet, dark places within, far from the noise and distraction of daily life. Its nature is descent.

Crossing the Spiritual Desert

Let's say you're cruising along in life, the wind is at your back, all the lights are green and all systems are "Go!"

In times such as this, it's as though you've tapped into a magical force, as every choice you make, every action you take manifests beyond your expectations. Life seems effortless as if you've finally learned the steps to the great cosmic dance of the universe. No more doubt and hesitation, no more confusion and uncertainty, just clear skies and smooth sailing ahead. Your relationships are full and nourishing, creative ideas flow, work is satisfying, opportunities abound. Your cup is filled to the brim and overflowing. Life doesn't get better.

You might even become overconfident and take one hand off the wheel, ease up on the gas, put the top down and let the wind blow through your hair. You put your life on cruise control, knowing you're in the "groove" and your momentum will carry you to wherever you're going.

Life seems too good to be true. That thought might even cross your mind. As in, *"Wow, I wonder how long this can last?"* But you dismiss that thought as life's goodness just keeps coming and you're enjoying the ride.

And then, so gradually that you barely notice, subtle shifts occur. That new client you thought you'd landed becomes hesitant, the payment you were expecting is delayed, your significant other gets cranky, those creative juices dry up and new opportunities appear out of reach.

You hardly notice that, while the wind was blowing through your hair and you were on cruise control enjoying the ride, your life went into neutral and your forward momentum slowed.

Even as you lose momentum, you have a set of good stories and excuses to entertain and distract your mind, and for a while you don't even notice the change. From where you're looking, everything still seems to be moving in the right direction.

What you fail to see here is you've taken your foot off the gas and your hands off the wheel. You became so distracted by the scenery you didn't see the sign that warned, "Sharp curve ahead" or "Fork in the road".

Ever so gradually, those green lights turn yellow, your momentum slows, and one day, the yellow lights turn red and you come to a dead stop. You find yourself deposited at the doorstep of what seems like a vast desert.

You might not even know you're here at first. The mind, in its infinite capacity to escape reality, holds on to the fantasy that everything is still working. All systems are "go". It could be your body that acts like the canary in the coal mine and eventually lets you know all is not well. Insomnia, digestion or elimination problems might be the first clues that something is off.

You become aware you feel empty and dry. Your veil of denial is ripped away. Your attention is finally engaged and you realize that one more time, you've fallen asleep at the wheel of your life, a humbling awareness.

Welcome to the spiritual desert, a vast interior terrain that at first glance, appears to be foreboding territory. This isn't the first time you've found yourself here. You're familiar with this place. The last time you visited, you resisted being here. It doesn't look like an exciting place to be.

No welcome mat is spread. No juice bars in sight. No cool, shady places to stop and rest. And it looks like you're out here in the wilderness alone and unprepared for the journey. You have no camping equipment, nothing to sit on or keep you warm. You left your GPS behind, there's no Wi-Fi or Internet connection out here and there are no familiar landmarks.

You search for something to give you a sense of direction, but you see no signposts. The sun has set, and the sky is dark, devoid of stars. You might as well be on the moon and wonder if you are. No doubt about it. You are seriously off track. No, actually, you're lost.

I think you get the picture. Let me be the first to admit that I've traveled this road many times in my 76 years on the planet. Each time I finally realize it, I vow it will be the last.

But such a vow is a foolish denial of the human journey and the spiritual work we're all required to do. Even Christ spent time in the wilderness. Who am I to believe I could avoid a similar fate?

If we are here to evolve, to deepen and expand our idea of who we are and contribute to the transformation of our collective human experience, we must do the work that is required of us. Namely, we must shed the old skins and let go of our limiting beliefs about who we are and why we're here. To do that, our soul requires that we periodically "take ourselves to the wood shed" and do remedial work. Also known as, you guessed it, going Beyond the Box!

When the ego gets too big for its britches and we lose our humility, the soul has a way of serving up just the right remedy. Not punishment. Not that we're wrong. Just off track. And if you've committed yourself to being a servant of truth, the truth will ultimately set you free. You just need to undo the chains that bind you to whatever false notion of truth brought you to the desert to get your attention. When you find yourself in the spiritual desert, here are some things to remember:

Know you are in an important soul process. Trust it. The soul doesn't mess around. It comes with an agenda to fulfill, namely the life curriculum and accompanying lessons you signed up for when you took a physical body. You may return to the main road when you've done your work. So get busy.

Surrender. Surrender doesn't mean you give up. It simply means you stop resisting what is. By resisting, you will only prolong your stay in the desert. To truly surrender is to be in a very high state of consciousness wherein you give yourself permission to be right where you are. You're here, aren't you? If you were supposed to be elsewhere, you would be. Surrender is an active state of awareness that requires your full attention and ability to be present here and now. Surrender and invite your ego to join you.

Get still. Become silent and listen. Set aside all your agenda, let go of your strategies and game plans and open yourself to receive guidance from a higher source. Don't force it. In the silence will come the guidance you desire.

Pay attention to your dreams. Dreams are the language of the soul. Put pen and paper next to your bed and before turning out the light, ask for a dream that will help you know what to do next. Be sure to record your dreams upon awakening. Imagine your dream as a story in which you are all the characters. What do the various parts of the dream suggest to you about your journey?

Keep a journal. Record your process. Give your subconscious mind a chance to download its content and step back. This is a goldmine of information to explore. Here, you'll find clues for how to make your way through the darkness.

Notice the edges where growth is possible. Even one small change in the system changes the entire system. What one, small change can you make?

Take action toward your higher wisdom and guidance. This one action will itself cause a shift in the system. Keep taking new actions even if you can't see the outcome yet.

Trust the process. Suddenly you'll realize you're awake! That's the point! Now you can see a path through the desert and beyond. You might see many paths leading to new territories beyond.

Choose one and begin the next part of your journey.

Enjoy the ride! But remember, going on cruise control can lull you back to sleep, so consider keeping your hands on the wheel and foot on the gas and put your life on "Conscious Steering" instead.

Caution:

Don't be surprised if you find yourself in the desert more than once in your life. If you do, don't waste time fretting about being there. It's part of the process. The sooner you accept your fate, the sooner you can evolve yourself.

I don't mean to suggest that navigating the desert is as simple as 1-2-3. It can take years to make one trip to and through. In my lifetime, I've spent nine consecutive years in my own spiritual desert. When I look back on that period of my life, I now see it as having been a necessary part of my soul journey.

Without the learning that came out of the experience, I wouldn't be the person I am today. It was painful, but the pain I experienced taught me about my own humanity. It taught me to accept my vulnerability, how to be compassionate and humble. I learned my own value and worthiness. I learned how to love myself and became an adult.

The soul will surely have its way with us. When it takes you to the desert, sit up straight and pay attention. The teacher has arrived and class is about to begin. And take notes. As we learn to work *with* the soul instead of *against* it, life gets easier. The events don't get easier; we simply get better at dealing with and learning from them.

Food for Thought

- What patterns do you observe about your journey?

- What relationship issues reappear with different people?

- What is your soul attempting to teach you?

- What is your soul's agenda?

- How have you resisted your soul's agenda?

- How can you cooperate with your soul?

CHAPTER SIX

The Addiction to Certainty

One morning while riding along the bike path to San Francisco's Ocean Beach, I noticed a sign posted in the sand warning beach goers of dangerous rip tides in the area. The sign read, "Remain Safely on Shore".

Good advice for surfers and swimmers, but it made me think about how much energy human beings spend avoiding risks and clinging to the shore of what is known or predictable. It is human nature to avoid pain and seek certainty. We are descendants of those smart, clever, and fast enough to avoid being eaten, as survival skills are programmed into our DNA.

While we no longer need to worry we'll end up as dinner for wild beasts like our earliest ancestors did, today we have other challenges to face. We live in extraordinary times that demand different skills to meet life in this twenty-first century. With global warming and climate change, drought and water shortages, rising energy prices, stagnating employment, low wages and the war on terror, we live in a time when our old assumptions no longer apply. We are in the midst of tsunami-sized change, and it's a challenging ride to be alive today!

How do you get enough courage to leave the safe shore and head into the open seas if it's your first time to steer the ship called "your life"? No wonder so many young people live in their parents' basements! Talk about safety! For many, this strategy is their only answer. But is it?

When the unexpected happens and you're thrown off course, the first reaction is usually strong emotions; panic, fear, anxiety or depression. Old patterns, self-limiting beliefs and conditioning get activated. The mind cautions that you've managed to get yourself this far. Why change now? This is how you've learned to survive. Stay with what you know. Better stay safe than be sorry, right?

In a world of rapid change these reactions have protected you and helped to maintain an illusion of safety. They've defined your comfort zone. But they've kept you stuck there.

It's not pleasant, this place called "stuck". If you stay there long enough, you'll eventually give up hope that your life might ever change. After you've given up hope, the cascade of emotions takes you on a downward spiral through anxiety, depression, fear or indifference and you end up at "lost".

It's even bleaker at lost than at stuck. At least when you were stuck, you still had a sense of your bearings. You weren't happy there, but you could sense the floor and the walls and tell if you were upright or not.

But lost? Stuck looks good compared to lost. When you're lost, all bets are off. You don't know which way to turn. There might be wake-up opportunities, but you'll miss them.

Days, weeks, months or even years could pass, but when you've had enough of being lost you'll finally start to get restless and look for the exits. Then, the strangest thing happens. You'll find an exit where you thought there was none.

This isn't a miracle. Fear, anxiety and depression are powerful blinders that can keep us from seeing possibilities when they're right in front of us. Life is always guiding us towards the experiences we need to shake us up and wake us up. So when we're ready for the exit door, we'll find it.

A wake-up call will sound, and when it does, it's your job to answer. If you don't, it will sound again, and with more intensity next time. And if you continue to ignore, avoid or deny the call, life will keep on calling you until you wake up. Or die, whichever comes first. In your case, let's hope it's the former and not the latter. That's why you're reading this book, right?

The call often comes as trauma or loss. It might show up as a medical or health crisis, death, divorce, or a relationship breakdown. We think it comes from "left field", but that's only how it looks in the physical realm.

When the road takes a sudden swerve and you're thrown off course, consider this experience was necessary to have you wake up, get going, and get serious about the business of creating your life.

You might struggle with this idea. Many people resist and insist these circumstances are not of their making. You may think you're a victim and powerless to change. As long as you stay in this mentality, nothing will change and you'll stay stuck for a while longer.

I know this idea might not fit into your current level of consciousness, but remember what Albert Einstein counseled, "Problems can never be solved from the same mindset that created them." You must "think outside the box" to get beyond your current circumstances.

When at last you wake up and accept that you are the source of your experience and the creator of your life instead of the victim, the real work can begin. Here are some steps to take AFTER the wake-up call has landed and life has your full attention.

Stop everything. Quit doing whatever you did that wasn't working. Quiet the mind chatter and inner voices that tell you what a loser you are, that you'll never amount to anything, or why even start since you know you'll fail. Stop the unproductive behavior you've been using to avoid your life. Substance abuse, including alcohol, drugs, food, TV, shopping, Internet, video games, or hanging out with your friends, can be distractions to avoid knowing the truth about yourself and your life right now. No more avoiding! Stop and tune in to what's happening at ground zero.

Look. Step back, assess your current situation and determine your options for moving ahead. There are always more available options than you think, so face your fear, look beyond it and be willing to discover new possibilities for productive action.

Give up the need for certainty and embrace change as the prevailing context of our time. To cling to the illusion of certainty is not a winning strategy when 98% of what happens is outside your control.   Get comfortable being uncomfortable and know that the 2% you can control, matters. You can resist what's in front of you or you can embrace it.

Develop your courage muscles by doing something every day that scares the heck out of you. What would you do if you knew you couldn't fail?

Choose. Consider your available options, and choose one. Instead of choosing what's safe, familiar and comfortable, choose a possibility to act upon that stretches and empowers you. Choose a possibility that opens new doors and invites you into questions that lead to new discoveries. Choose to risk expanding your comfort zone, choose to risk looking foolish or even failing. Choose to shed old beliefs and move beyond your fear. You'll never know if you never do it. So do it! Meaning …

Take action. Take action based on making the choice that empowers and inspires you to move forward. Be willing to be wrong, but also be willing to be amazed and inspired by how far you can go if you give yourself permission. Get committed and get started. Life is short, and the clock keeps running. What in your life matters enough for you to risk looking foolish or worse yet, making a "mistake"? Mistakes are the universe's cosmic "time outs".

Mistakes are where the learning happens, so don't be afraid of making them. When your commitment is bigger than your fear, you become unstoppable. There are bigger fish to fry than playing small and staying safe. You came to use your life in service to a larger purpose.

Discover your vision and purpose and then live them with gusto. To stay on course requires that you know where you intend to go. A vision for your life and a sense of purpose invite you to be larger than your fear, limiting beliefs or the obstacles that appear on the path. Together, your vision and purpose serve as your North Star. They're something to true up to when you've lost your way.

Develop your gifts. Once you've discovered your purpose and discovered your unique gifts, give them away. Use them to serve a purpose larger than yourself. What is the world you want to pass on to your children and grandchildren?

Turbulent times invite us to become stronger, wiser, calmer, and clearer. Swim out into the waters of your life. Summon your courage and commitment and use your vision and purpose as your compass. Swim to a distant shore you can't see from where you are and discover yourself anew. Discover the one in you who is magnificent and whole. Expand the shoreline of your Being, so your definition of "safe haven" is you! Your destiny awaits and you are here to fulfill it.

Food for Thought

Use a large sheet of paper, pens, colored pencils or crayons to do the following:

Draw a line that represents your life's journey, starting with birth and going right up to the present time.

See your life unfolding like a movie. Chart the twists and turns, ups and downs. Notice where you circled back came to a dead end and started over.

- On this line, mark the significant events that have occurred in your life. Make an X, and place a note beside it, identifying what happened and the approximate date.

- As the line goes upward, recall what was happening at that time. How did you feel?

- As the line goes down, what was happening? What were you feeling?

- If you remember a major event later, go back to your lifeline and include it.

- This "Lifeline" is a map of your life. Refer to it throughout the chapters that follow.

- Feel free to make notes about what you learned from these experiences as the lessons become apparent to you.

CHAPTER SEVEN

Kick Up Your Courage

I f you're going to "Lean Out, Break Free and Rise Up!" you'll need to develop your courage muscles. How to do that? Instead of moving *away* from the things that scare you, move *towards* those things you resist. In other words, do something every day that scares the heck out of you. Obviously, this must not be as simple as it sounds or everyone would already have broken through their fears and be well on the road to fulfilling their potential and living their best lives.

We already looked at how to make friends with your fear. That's the first step in building courage. Let's look beyond and see what's next.

When I suggest you do something scary on a daily basis, I don't mean you should step in front of a bus or put yourself at physical risk, although if the idea of bungee jumping or sky diving appeals to you, go for it! If you've ever taken an outdoor challenge course, you've experienced what can happen to your self-esteem and self-confidence as a result of facing your fears and going beyond what you thought you could do. Outdoor challenges are one way to develop your courage muscles. But there are many ways to develop courage and build self-confidence to help you face your life head on.

What if you saw your life as an adventure instead of something to endure? What if you could see that exploding the box and coloring outside the lines could reap enormous rewards?

When you visit a foreign country or go to a place you've never been, your everyday patterns get disrupted and nothing is predictable. You don't know what's around the next corner, but your curiosity is stronger than your fear, so you go for it anyway. You try new things, eat foods you've never eaten, climb to the top of a temple, meet new people and make new friends. What if you could approach your everyday life with that same attitude?

In 1999, I began leading seminars in Taipei, Taiwan, spending three out of every six weeks there. My work was concentrated into two weeks, with a week in between. Rather than fly back and forth, it was more cost effective to have a place of my own, so my hosts rented an apartment for me and other trainers to use. It made my life much easier!

On the week in between trainings, my time was my own, and one of my favorite things to do was to get acquainted with the area around my apartment. Every morning I would set out walking on a different route. My *intention* was to lose my way. Why? So that I could practice confronting my fears of being lost in a foreign place, not speaking the language and therefore feeling completely out of control. And so I could also practice trusting myself and listening to my intuition in figuring out how to find my way back home. I considered these my little daily exploding the box "Dorothy" practices. I definitely wasn't in Kansas anymore!

Taipei is filled with thousands of small streets and back alleys that intersect and bisect at unpredictable angles. Every tiny alleyway is filled with shops and restaurants, and to my Western eyes, they all looked the same. It wasn't hard to get lost!

Back then, there were no smartphones or GPSs available to "cheat" and help me always know where I was. Those "lost" experiences were filled with adventures I remember to this day. There were few Western people in those back streets and alleys. Most stuck close to the major hotels and main shopping areas. I suppose that's why I was often a point of curiosity for the locals. Often they wanted to practice their English and tried to engage in a few words of polite conversation.

Other encounters were more mysterious. One day, I was walking down a sidewalk in an area I'd never been in before and looked out in front of me to see an elderly man with long white hair and a long white beard approaching me, head on. We kept walking towards each other and I wondered who would be the first one to shift to the left or right. We got to about three feet apart when he stopped abruptly and bowed to me. My response was to bow back at him. He motioned me to go inside a shop in front of which we happened to be standing. It was a shop that sold large paintings, mostly of Chinese landscapes, and of course, statues of Buddha.

This elderly gentleman didn't speak a word to me and proceeded to take me on a tour of the paintings, pointing to this one and that one, and I smiled and nodded my approval and delight in being given a personally guided tour by a total stranger. When we completed the tour, we arrived back at the entrance to the shop. Once again, he bowed to me and I to him. He turned and walked back down the street in the direction from which he'd come. Not a word was exchanged between us.

What was I to make of that experience? Was it the universe's way of confirming my desire to have an adventure? Surely this never would have occurred if I'd stayed inside my apartment or walked a block away to pick up some food at the local market. Or would it? Who knows?

The truth is: every day is a new moment. You have never walked on the territory of this day before. It could be like every other day, in which you show up being who you've always been, doing what you've always done and creating the same results you've always had. Or you could wake up into the thought: "Today is a brand new day. I've never lived this day before. What could be possible?"

If you can see your life through the lens of adventure your antennae will be in the up position. New possibilities become visible. Embrace the spirit of adventure and you'll begin to see new solutions to old problems. The impossible begins to look possible. You'll learn to tap into resources you didn't know you had, like courage for starters.

So exactly how do you go about building up your courage? Here are a few suggestions:

Give yourself daily "Beyond the Box" stretch assignments

A stretch is the opposite of a break. It's you choosing to go beyond your comfort zone and doing what's uncomfortable. Start with small stretches and work up to the bigger ones. Make a game of it. What would be a stretch for you?

Some examples:

- Take yourself out to dinner and eat alone at a busy restaurant
- Take a dance class
- Join Toastmasters and learn public speaking
- Study a new language

- Travel to a foreign country by yourself

- Approach a difficult person at work

- Ask for a raise

- Share with your boss your great new ideas for increasing productivity in the workplace

Clean up your relationships

Addressing relationship breakdowns is the biggest source of avoidance for most people. If you have relationship issues with someone, stop waiting for them to take the first step towards making amends. Be proactive! Get busy and clean it up.

Who are the people in your life with whom you have unfinished business? Misunderstandings, hurt feelings, dishonesty, lack of trust, and betrayal sit like stones in the heart. When the heart is heavy with unexpressed painful emotions, we are stopped dead in our tracks. This is how we perpetuate being stuck.

If you're afraid to tell the truth to someone important in your life, start there. Withholding honesty kills intimacy and plants the seeds for disrespect to grow instead of love.

It takes courage to face up to these breakdowns. But address them you must if your life is to move ahead. This is the next level of "stretching". Even though it might be difficult and scary to be honest when you've withheld the truth, it's your own integrity that's at stake.

You don't know what will happen if you tell the truth, but you know what will happen if you don't. No new risks, no new results. What you have to lose is your false sense of pride and the illusion of being right.

Give up the need to look good

This is a deadly quality guaranteed to keep you in your box and shrink your courage muscles. Worrying about what other people will think or say if you express yourself authentically may help you to fit in, but it comes with a price.

It's not wrong to want to fit in. At some level, everyone wants and needs to fit in and look normal. But it's important to be clear about the price we pay for doing so. If you compromise your integrity or authenticity in order to look good and fit in, who loses in the end? If you stifle your creativity, and give up your personal power in order to fit in, is it worth it?

The need to look good at all costs kills courage. How can you take risks if you feel you need to be perfect? Olympic athletes strive for perfection, but they also take enormous risks. Sometimes they win and sometimes they fail. But failures are where the learning happens. Let go of needing to look good and give yourself permission to make mistakes and be wrong. This leaves room for learning. It allows for freedom and passion, which are both strong courage builders.

Trust that you are enough

Know that you can count on you to come through, no matter what. You don't have to be perfect; but isn't it good to know that whether the chips are down or they're up, you will be there for yourself? Even if you have no idea how to accomplish your goals or go after your dreams, there is a deeper well of wisdom from which to draw. Trust that you can draw from it when you need it.

Be a "YES"!

Yes, you can. Yes, you will. Say yes, not because you need someone's approval, but because in your heart you know that being a "yes" to life opens the doors to new adventures that will take you to places you never dreamed.

Make a game out of saying yes to something every day that makes you uncomfortable. What would you do if you knew you couldn't fail? Your courage waits for you. What will you say "yes" to today?

Food for Thought

- Commit to doing one thing every day for a week that scares you. What stretches do you commit to doing this week?

- When those start to feel comfortable, do some more.

- Remember, in order to be effective as courage "kicker uppers", your actions need to be ones that challenge your need to stay comfortable and maintain the status quo.

- What stretch will you take today?

CHAPTER EIGHT

When the Mind Has a Mind of Its Own

I f our intention is to learn how to thrive in chaotic times, it becomes paramount that we learn how let go of the past. Clinging to our old, worn-out beliefs and ideas about how life works and who we are in the matter no longer serves. It's time for a radical upgrade in our physical, mental, emotional and spiritual software, i.e. the operating system of the mind.

In order to effect that kind of change on a personal level, we need to take a deep dive into our own subconscious mind and discover what lies in that territory. For everything we see in the visible has its roots in the invisible. Here's what I mean:

Iceberg Analogy

Think of an iceberg. We can see about 10% of an iceberg above the water line. Therefore, approximately 90% of that iceberg lies below the water line, invisible to the naked eye.

We can use this analogy to study human beings. We're a lot like an iceberg. What lies in the visible realm of human being, how we show up in the world, the results we create, the state of our relationships, the status of our health, our relationship with money, our job and career results, etc. all are in the 10% above the water line. This is the realm of our conscious awareness. We tend to think of the conscious mind as that part of us that is in charge, the part of us that makes our decisions and choices and charts our path through life.

It might appear to be that way, but this is not actually the case. For when we consider that 90% of our awareness lies below the water line in the realm of the subconscious and that we cannot see and do not know what lies within it, we begin to see where the real power lies. It's in the subconscious mind. Ninety percent of our choices, decisions and actions are dictated by what lies hidden from view. Knowing this, it becomes critical to begin the work of diving into this inner realm and discovering what we do not know that we do not know. And what we'll find is that the mind has a mind of its own. Let's take a deeper look.

Have you ever created a result or an outcome opposite from what you said you wanted? Of course you have! But what's that about? What's going on when you say you intend do one thing, but you end up doing something completely different?

You might tell yourself you want to lose weight and you commit to shedding ten pounds. You diet and go to the gym and work out. But at the end of six months, not only did you not lose any weight you; might even have gained a few pounds. Or you might lose weight, but after a short time you gain it right back. What is that about? What is going on? Remember, the mind has a mind of its own.

Say you decide you want to get your finances under control. You've been hemorrhaging money, frittering it away on things you don't need and can't afford. So you tell yourself you intend to learn to live within your means. For a few months, you budget your money wisely. But within six months, your credit card balances have returned to their maxed-out levels, and you are right back to your old habits. What is that about? What is going on?

Or maybe you realize you need more balance in your life. You work long hours and come home so tired and exhausted you're not available to spend quality time with your family. Your relationships might be suffering, or your health is compromised because you're working too much and not taking care of yourself. You tell yourself you need to get a grip on your priorities and get serious about having more balance in your life. And for a few weeks you succeed. But after a while, you fall back into your old patterns, and nothing has changed. What is that really about?

Is it possible to change old habits and patterns, or are you forever doomed to fail? And if it is possible, how do you go about doing it?

Consider that based on results, in every area of your life, you get exactly what you intend to have – no more, no less. This is an important awareness in understanding how to change your results.

How is it possible for your results to reflect a different intention than the one you say you intend? The answer to this question sounds simple at first glance. When we don't have the results we say we intend, it's because something else is more important. "But no," you say. "Nothing is more important! Losing weight/saving money/spending more time with family/taking care of my health is the most important priority in my life!" You might think so, but based on results, it's not so. How do I know? Your results never lie. And remember, the mind has a mind of its own. Here's how this works:

Consider the story of Elizabeth. She is in her 60s, overweight, and wants to lose 50 pounds. When she was 11 years old, a family member sexually molested Elizabeth. This started a cycle of repeated sexual assaults that lasted well into her teen years. The person who molested her told her she was "very sexy". At such a young age, Elizabeth didn't understand what being "sexy" even meant, except she sensed it wasn't a good thing. She felt ashamed and blamed herself, so she told no one what happened. Because being seen as "sexy" brought her pain, by her late teen years, Elizabeth decided, at a subconscious level, it was better to hide her sexiness than risk more sexual violations. So she put on weight.

To make sure she was safe, Elizabeth packed on the pounds and still struggles with her weight. Today, she acknowledges she has gained and lost the same 50 pounds many times. Each time she loses weight, she experiences those old memories of being "cute and sexy", and her fear of being hurt is alive and well, just as it was when she was a teenager.

Even though Elizabeth says she wants to lose those 50 pounds, her subconscious belief says something else. This belief tells her it's not safe to lose weight and if she did, she might get hurt again. Elizabeth can't lose the weight and keep it off because at a subconscious level, she believes it's better to be fat and safe than sexy and in pain.

Beyond how she looks or how much she weighs, Elizabeth is a dynamic and vibrant woman. She's intelligent and caring, has a sparkle in her eyes and a smile that can light up a room. Those qualities are magnetic and attractive in anyone. One could say being dynamic and vibrant is "sexy"! Elizabeth can't run away from who she is, no matter how much she weighs or how old she is. She is a woman who commands people's attention in a positive way.

To break the cycle of continuing to carry the excess weight, Elizabeth needs to embrace the vibrant being she is. Her excess weight does not and cannot hide her best qualities, and it's those qualities that draw people to her. Elizabeth doesn't need the extra weight anymore. When she was young, the weight protected her, but today she has grown beyond needing its protection.

In order for Elizabeth to lose weight, she must first acknowledge how she used it for protection when she didn't have the wisdom, maturity or outer resources to help her confront her issues around the sexual molestation. Today, Elizabeth is taking back her personal power. She no longer needs to be a victim of anyone else's ideas about her sexuality.

Like Elizabeth, we all carry around subconscious beliefs that often come from childhood and limit our ability to be present, here and now. Based on our childhood experiences, we might believe we're not worthy of being loved, or that life is a struggle, or that we're not enough, or that we need to protect ourselves because the world isn't a safe place. To the degree those beliefs live in the subconscious, they become the operating system that determines and influences the choices we make today. And even if, at the conscious level, we say we want one thing, if our subconscious beliefs are in conflict, they will rule the day.

How can we learn which subconscious beliefs keep us stuck? Begin by looking at your results. When we say one thing but create a different result, a subconscious, conflicting belief is at work.

Our beliefs can either support us to open and grow, or keep us stuck in the status quo. The key is to realize what purpose the conflicting subconscious belief is serving. What are you getting from it that is more important than having the results you say you want? Consider these benefits:

Protection and safety

Elizabeth's extra weight gave her protection. It allowed her to hide her sexuality and be safe. Protection and safety were much more important to her than losing weight even though she said losing weight is what she wanted.

We get to be right

But what's the payoff for not having enough time, money, education, intimacy or good health? How could these conditions produce a reward? If you harbor an unconscious belief that you don't deserve money or are unworthy of love or success, you won't create it in the material world. No matter what you say, you'll sabotage yourself and your results. And what is the payoff of self-sabotage? You'll get to be right about what you believe to be true. We'll do anything to be right, including sabotaging our ability to get what we say we want.

We get to avoid pain

If you believe you're not worthy of love, that no one wants to be with you, or, if they do, they always leave, an intimate, close relationship sounds painful. Why risk being hurt if you're convinced pain is what you'll get? Why even try? You might think the pain of loneliness is safer than the pain of a broken heart. At least if you're lonely, you can keep it to yourself and no one else needs to know. This is what you tell yourself. But what's the truth here? Pain is pain, no matter the source. You're not avoiding anything. Instead, you keep the illusion of control.

What's the solution? What can you do to move from a pattern of consistent self-sabotage and results that contradict those which you say you want?

Do the inner work necessary to discover what's driving your results at the subconscious level. This inner work takes courage. It requires you to face up to your fears and be honest with yourself. It's difficult, if not impossible, to solve one's problems from inside the same box in which they were created.

Find someone who can help you see beyond what you can see, and see what you can't see. As suggested in an earlier chapter of this book, you might seek a counselor, a therapist or a coach or join a mastermind group to help you tackle what might be deeply embedded, subconscious beliefs. Remember, the solutions lie outside the box. Exploding that box becomes paramount if you are to breakthrough and move forward.

Breaking through old patterns takes courage, commitment and a willingness to see yourself with new eyes. If you're confronted with conflicting results, ask yourself, "What's more important than having what I say I want?" Don't settle for a good story or an excuse. Take responsibility and be willing to look deeper and know the truth.

I contend life occurs just the way we order it. Our words, thoughts, actions and beliefs work together to order up the results we're creating. You can use your power to break the hold of those old habits and patterns. When you discover you are the source of your own safety, worthiness, abundance and love, and you are 100-percent responsible for creating your life, you will no longer need the excuses or benefits your limiting beliefs provided, and a new life of freedom, passion and aliveness awaits!

Food for Thought

- What patterns have kept you stuck?

- What limiting beliefs have you held that are responsible for you having exactly what you have?

- What benefits do these beliefs provide?

- How can you reap those benefits and let go of the old behaviors?

CHAPTER NINE

Learning to Love Uncertainty

"I wanted a perfect ending. Now I've learned, the hard way,
that some poems don't rhyme, and some stories don't have a clear
beginning, middle, and end. Life is about not knowing, having
to change, taking the moment and making the best of it, without
knowing what's going to happen next. Delicious ambiguity."

Gilda Radner

Remember Gilda Radner of Saturday Night Live fame? Was she onto something? "Delicious ambiguity"? Sounds like a good definition for "cognitive dissonance". Two words that normally don't go together are put together to suggest an entirely new and different possibility. It's like Chinese sweet and sour soup. What could be more delicious? Let's take a look:

Ambiguity is not something one usually courts. In fact, most people detest the idea. Ambiguity is akin to uncertainty, and we all know that uncertainty is fraught with danger. At least we've been conditioned to think that way.

In fact, we humans will go a long way to eliminate ambiguity and uncertainty from our lives. We want to sweep the decks of anything that is undefined and vague. Stock markets do not rally on uncertainty. Neither do most people.

Except Gilda. She knew something, or at least if she didn't start out knowing it, she learned it along the way. And that's the thing about uncertainty and perhaps the reason it might serve us to deem it "delicious." Because inside uncertainty, nothing has yet taken form and therefore, all things are possible. Who wouldn't find being in a field of infinite possibility a delicious experience? Most people don't, but guess what? We find ourselves in such a field every moment. Yet most of us reject the notion that uncertainty can be a "delicious" experience. And why do we reject it? Because we are more like Goldilocks than Gilda.

We want life to come in just the right portions. We don't want it to be too hot or too cold. We don't want a life so big we can't get our arms wrapped around it and end up feeling out of control. We also don't want a life that's too small, one that cramps our creativity with too little stimulation or too few opportunities for growth. And, like Gilda, we want a happy ending.

We don't want surprises, like losing a job or a relationship, or even worse. We want certainty and predictability, and we want life to make sense. We want life to unfold in a linear fashion, so we know where we are in the story and can expect what's coming next.

Prior to 9/11, Americans lived in the fantasy that we had control of our lives. Now, this was never actually true, but we preferred the narrative of control and certainty to that of chaos and unpredictability. And then everything changed.

After 9/11 and the economic meltdown of 2008, all bets were off. We may still long for the "good old days" where at least we still had our illusions of certainty, but today, even the illusions are gone.

Life has always been uncertain. The only difference is that today we can no longer entertain the illusion that it's anything else. We now live in the great cauldron of uncertainty and are learning how to swim in its waters. How are you doing?

Given this "new" reality – not new, except that our collective awareness has shifted and we're now realizing that the game has permanently changed – how best to proceed from here? If there is no solid ground on which to stand, what kind of beings do we need to become in order to dwell in the land of uncertainty and learn to reap its potential rewards?

Gilda's theory of life gives us a clue. Start with changing your mind. What if your old way of thinking about uncertainty was not wrong but outdated and in need of a makeover?

The newest discoveries in quantum physics are causing scientists to rethink everything we once believed to be true. What if uncertainty could be viewed as a field of infinite possibilities and "delicious ambiguity" instead of scary and overwhelming? How would changing your mind change your receptivity about living with uncertainty? What consciousness would empower you to be most effective?

If you weren't frightened by uncertainty, but open to its possibilities, it would change everything. And if you can change your mind about this, what other untruths held as truths could use a makeover? How many times have you updated the software on your computer or completely changed operating systems? Doesn't your life require and deserve at least that level of attention? What worked for your life 20 or 30 years ago is most likely due for an update.

Gilda advises that we make the best of each moment. Or, as author Gregg Braden says: "The happiest people don't have the best of everything. They make the best of everything they have."

This isn't anything new or revolutionary. But do you put this into practice? Making the most of each moment requires that we show up for it as our awakened, aware selves. It requires that we not be attached to how the moment unfolds or the outcome, but be willing participants in the here and now, meeting the moment as it is, open to surprise and unpredictability.

Gilda Radner's life did not have a happy ending. She died of ovarian cancer at age 43 after being misdiagnosed for ten months, during which she struggled with extreme pain and discomfort. She once quipped, "I joined a club I didn't want to belong to." Even Gilda had a hard time living by her own hard-earned wisdom.

> *"No one imagines that a symphony is supposed to improve in quality as it goes along, or that the whole object of playing it is to reach the finale. The point of music is discovered in every moment of playing and listening to it. It is the same with the greater part of our lives ... And if we are absorbed in improving them, we may forget altogether to live them."*

Allen Watts

The one thing that's certain is this present moment. What are you bringing to this one, uncivilized, elegant moment of your life? How can you bring a sense of delicious presence to this ambiguous possibility called Now?

Food for Thought

- What old beliefs and untruths have you held on to that are now due for a makeover?

- What would be possible if you changed your mind about them?

- How would your relationships be impacted?
  Your health? Career?

- What will it take for you to let go, and change your mind?

CHAPTER TEN

The Power of
"Conscious Forgetting"

O ne of the reasons we stay lost and stuck and fail to learn how to adapt to the turbulence of these times is because we keep recycling the past and can never get beyond it. We get stuck in our stories about what happened and what it meant and what we'll never allow to happen again. We'd rather be right about our old stories than investigate other possibilities for how to view them, get the lessons they came to teach us, give them up and move on.

How does one get out of that cycle and get on with life? In her 1992 bestselling book, *Women Who Run With The Wolves*, Jungian analyst, Dr. Clarissa Pinkola Estes introduced a phenomenon she called, Conscious Forgetting. She explains:

"Conscious forgetting does not mean to make yourself brain-dead, it means letting go of the event, to not insist it stay in the foreground, but rather allow it to be relegated to the background or move off stage. We practice conscious forgetting by refusing to summon up the fiery emotional material. We refuse to recollect. To consciously forget is an active, not a passive, endeavor. It means to not haul up certain materials, or turn them over and over, to not work oneself up by repetitive thought, picture, or emotion. Conscious forgetting means willfully dropping the practice of obsessing, not looking back, thereby living in a new landscape, creating new life and new experiences to think about instead of the old ones. This kind of forgetting does not erase memory, it lays the emotion surrounding the memory to rest."

Dr. Estes' conscious forgetting suggests that we not repress painful memories, but rather allow the emotion surrounding them to dissipate by "refusing to recollect the fiery material", the emotional impact, which is self-inflicted and divorced from the painful event itself.

The event does not cause the emotion. We bring the emotional response, or reaction, to the event. This is an important distinction to remember, but admittedly, a difficult one to access in the heat of the experience.

By our nature as humans, we give meaning to what happens in our lives. When we recall an event, we don't just recall the bare facts about it, we also recall the raw emotional impact that occurred for us at the time. We might not even remember the factual nature of what happened, who did what to whom, when, where, what time of day or night, etc. But we remember how we felt, and what we made of it. Our memories coalesce around the conclusions we make and the resulting decisions we forge out of what happens.

In other words, we live not out of what happens in our lives, the facts, but out of the stories, or interpretations, we tell ourselves about the facts. There is an enormous difference between the two and it is important to be able to distinguish one from the other.

For example, Terry, an accomplished and successful woman, though having left an abusive marriage years ago, still operates as if the next episode of abuse is just around the corner, waiting for her to display a character imperfection. Today, she has no freedom to be herself, out of a conditioned fear that others might judge her as lacking or missing the mark. Never mind that her record of accomplishments is a mile long, she is convinced that who she is, is flawed. Her emotional conditioning around the abuse is still so present in her memory, that although the abuse ended years ago, by keeping that memory alive and activated, she has become the source of her own continued self-abuse.

Even though she has a loving relationship with a man who adores her, she is unable to fully open and trust that his love could be authentic. She still keeps others at bay, trapped behind a wall of her own making so as to protect that which she feels is vulnerable, namely, her own heart.

Meanwhile, the heart of this beautiful woman wants to open. She wants to connect and be close, but doesn't know how to get beyond her conditioned response to years of abuse.

Conscious Forgetting = switching channels

Terry learned how to shift her focus from the emotional impact of the abuse, replaying the fear and sense of powerlessness, to recognizing and acknowledging the inner strength and courage she called upon to not only survive, but also to leave that abusive environment. This empowers her to call upon those same qualities today, and end her pattern of self-abuse. Consciously forgetting means to "change channels", from abuse to empowerment.

With ADHD and a lifelong learning challenge, Sarah graduated from law school, which was an accomplishment itself. With her dream to become a lawyer, she sat for the bar exam, but failed it. She took the exam again at the next opportunity. Again she failed, although by a smaller margin. Still determined, she took and failed the exam four times, each time inching in on the magic, passing score, but each time not quite hitting the mark. After the fourth failure, she was so traumatized by the experience she gave up. But only for a moment.

This woman is a warrior! For a warrior type, failure was not an option. Whatever it took to pass the bar, she was going to go the distance. Sarah took time off, and cleared her mind. She did yoga, rode her bike, took long walks, and got her body fit and strong. Then she started over, blank slate, unencumbered by her experience of the past. She set aside her feelings of humiliation and embarrassment at having failed and started studying for the bar again. On the fifth attempt, she passed!

Sarah is one spectacular advocate as a lawyer. One of her first tasks after passing the bar was to advocate for the establishment of new policy procedures around concessions for ADHD students taking the bar exam in her state. Her own failures helped pave the way and make it easier for others like her who followed. But only because she set aside her emotional baggage around failure and kept going. She had a dream and a clear vision for her life. Failure wouldn't keep her from getting to her goal. She found a way to succeed.

Conscious forgetting is a way to reframe one's experience and neutralize the emotional impact. It is not to deny or repress the reality that certain impacts exist, but rather it is the ability to "walk the razor's edge" of mental discipline, knowing that on either side of the edge are potential outcomes that may be daunting, yet consciously choosing not to engage them.

Rather, one chooses, with full powers of consciousness, to stay above the fray. One chooses not to empower the emotions but to keep one's sights on the next step. Consciously "forgetting" shifts the emphasis from the emotional impact of memories that closed possibilities in the past, to recalling what happened minus the "heat" of your interpretation, and choosing to empower yourself in the present.

Sarah focused on passing the bar, not her four failures. Terry learned how to open her heart, instead of defending and protecting it. She no longer gives her power to her past.

Conscious forgetting is not the "garden variety" forgetting in which we repress memories in an attempt to avoid dealing with them. In conscious forgetting, we are aware of the entire spectrum of possibilities around painful or challenging memories and choose not to engage with the fiery emotional material, which can derail us and keep us locked in a loop of reactivity and obsession.

Remaining aware that all potential outcomes are available, not deceiving yourself or pretending danger might not exist, you focus on what you are moving towards, not away from. Or as the guru Gangaji says: "Don't express it and don't repress it." This is a powerful edge to ride, a thin edge of awareness, requiring our full presence to navigate without falling off.

On a personal level, a few years ago, I found this method extremely helpful in my own journey. What started out looking like a routine event turned into the roller coaster from hell and conscious forgetting became my only ally.

In March of 2010, I went in for my first mammogram after undergoing lumpectomy surgery for breast cancer the previous July. I went expecting everything to go smoothly – just an easy zip in, zip out kind of procedure. That is not what happened.

Female readers know that mammograms can be painful at worst, uncomfortable at best. Men, imagine having your testicles smashed and spread out between two glass plates, then stand there holding your breath during a series of x-rays and you start to get the picture.

After the mammogram, I was asked to wait for a few moments while they took a look at the image to make sure they got it right. Fifteen minutes later, the technician called me back and announced I would need to have a magnification mammogram on the right breast.

"Fine", I thought. "No big deal. They want to have a closer look? Fine with me." I saw no red flags waving, heard no alarm bells ringing. Second mammogram in 20 minutes, and I'm back to the waiting room, where, true to the nature of its name, I waited awhile longer. Another fifteen minutes later, I'm called back for a third mammogram, this time with an ultrasound.

Looking back, I still didn't get alarmed. I was in the moment, free of thoughts, putting one foot in front of the other.

Into the ultrasound room I went. A new technician went about her job, putting on the warming gel and moving the ultrasound wand over my breast. Then she showed me something on the screen and said, "I'm going to get the radiologist who will come in and tell you what's going on." Then she left the room.

So that's what happened. Those are the facts. Then there's what my mind did with what happened.

As the door closed behind the ultrasound technician, the first alarm sounded! "Is something going on?" my mind asked. "Crap! Something IS going on! WHAT is going on?"

And then, for the next few seconds before the radiologist came in, my mind went into overdrive. "Oh, no! Not again! This can't be happening!" Denial was having its way with me.

My mind was racing towards the edge of the cliff and about to plunge over, when a more sane voice inside piped up, "Now just wait a minute, calm down. You can deal with this." I took a deep breath and was trying to pull myself together when the radiologist entered the room.

She picked up the ultrasound wand and found the "area of concern," which she pointed out to me on the screen. It was huge! It looked like the size of Texas! "We'll need to biopsy this to know for sure what it is," she said, matter-of-factly.

She continued talking. I could see her lips moving, but my mind was busy doing reruns of the past year: surgery, drainage tubes, hospitals, nurses, recovery, etc. It was not a picture I wanted to see, not then, when I was barely through the healing process from less than a year before. I started to lose it right there on the table, with the radiologist hovering over me.

No longer able to hold back my emotions, I burst into tears. The doctor was taken aback. I'm sure she didn't expect this outburst from her simple announcement that a biopsy was in order. What's the big deal? It's a biopsy! She probably prescribes several every day.

Except my mind sailed off both into the past and into the future and turned it into the worst possible outcome: mastectomy followed by chemotherapy, loss of hair, radiation, a long recovery, maybe even worse.

Dr. Radiologist stammered, "Um, well, of course, we don't have to schedule it today. You can talk to your doctor first and decide what you want to do. We could do an MRI, but I won't feel comfortable unless we do a biopsy."

The following six weeks were an opportunity to practice conscious forgetting. Due to my travel schedule, I waited five weeks to have the biopsy, then another wait for the results. Six weeks later, the outcome. Benign!

The dense, fibrocystic breast tissue I've had all my life was the culprit. Even though it's shown up on my mammograms for 35 years and never been cause for concern, it raised concern this time around because it "looked different." No doubt due to the reduction surgery I had on that side in order to achieve a modicum of symmetry, given the size of the lumpectomy I had on the other side.

Of course, the outcome matters. I am grateful to be on the other side of a clean biopsy. I am grateful that I didn't have to face all the scenarios my mind conjured up. I felt relieved and liberated from the mental holding pattern in which I was for those six weeks.

However, what matters as much as the outcome is what I learned in the process. I got to practice being with my mind and emotions in a way that not only served me to get through the period of uncertainty; it made me stronger.

I cannot say for sure how I would have responded to a different outcome. I can only imagine that after the initial shock wore off, I would have marshaled my inner resources to go through the experience and come out the other side with different lessons than the ones I learned. In the end, it's all about using whatever life serves up as part of the curriculum for learning.

Conscious forgetting had been anything but being in denial of the facts. Upon awakening each morning, my first thought went to the uncertain future. However, I simply chose not to engage with the sea of emotions accompanying this thought.

I was not in denial that these emotions existed and if so choosing, I could have allowed myself to be engulfed in them in a heartbeat. The best way I can describe the experience is like being in a constant state of meditation. Sitting calmly at the center, watching and allowing the movement of emotions or reactions to take place, without engaging them, staying instead in a kind of gentle, vigilant state.

The key is having the ability to be at choice about it. The "conscious" part of "conscious forgetting" is where the work lies. It requires that one expand their capacity to hold an experience without becoming it. In this, there is great freedom.

In the end, it always comes down to having the ability to consciously choose how we experience our lives. Life happens and we choose. How we choose and what we choose determine what we experience. We can be unconscious and navigate on automatic pilot, a passenger of our own lives. We can hope for the best, hope that life is kind and that we can manage to make it through relatively unscathed. This scenario will require us to live carefully and cautiously, sticking close to shore, never venturing too far beyond safe moorings, lest we be caught in a sudden storm. Or, as Dr. Estes invites us: "We can choose to know that we are mighty ships, built for these times. We can hoist our sails and venture out to sea. In the language of aviators and sailors, ours is to sail forward now, all balls out. Understand the paradox: If you study the physics of a waterspout, you will see that the outer vortex whirls far more quickly than the inner one. To calm the storm means to quiet the outer layer, to cause it, by whatever countervailing means, to swirl much less, to move more evenly to match the velocity of the inner, far less volatile core – till whatever has been lifted into such a vicious funnel falls back to Earth, lays down, is peaceable again. I hope you will write this on your wall: When a great ship is in harbor and moored, it is safe, there can be no doubt. But ... that is not what great ships are built for."

Clarissa Pinkola Estes, *Letter To A Young Activist During Troubled Times*

Know that you are indeed, a "great ship", built to withstand the gales that test your endurance. All that you need is already within. Your task is to discover the resources you already have to help you navigate the turbulent times that come along as part of life.

Stormy weather need not sink your ship. Remembering that to "forget" the outer swirling vortex of emotions, focusing instead on the calmer, peaceful core will help restore balance, not to mention sanity.

Food for Thought

- What thoughts or worries have hijacked your mind? Here's a chance to practice "conscious forgetting".

- Follow the instructions in this chapter and take it on, like a meditation. If your emotions threaten to derail you, breathe in peace and calmness and see those emotions evaporate like puffs of air.

- How can you take better care and be gentler with yourself? What self-care practices can you begin doing now?

- Tell yourself, "Nothing to do, nothing to undo. All is well."

- Continue this practice as often as needed to soothe the mind and calm the body.

CHAPTER ELEVEN

What's Hope Got To Do With It?

In the experience of being tossed about by the swirling winds of change or feeling stuck and lost and in search of the way forward, it's not uncommon to go through a stage of giving up hope that you will ever find your way.

Hopelessness is a dangerous state. It comes right before resignation in the downward spiral of emotions and once we reach that condition, we've dug ourselves into a deep, dark hole and it looks like there's no possibility for a way out.

So what is it about hope? Is hope useful, or a waste of time? Does hope give people anything to cling to, or is it like cotton candy, sweet and satisfying at the moment, but leaving one with nothing more than a sugar high in its aftermath?

Over the course of my life, I've spent a lot of time hoping for things. As a child, during the summer, I hoped for the sound of the ice cream man, bells jingling from the handles of his pedal-powered ice cream/bicycle, and like the Pied Piper, enticing the children in the neighborhood to beg their mom for a nickel to buy an ice cream bar before he disappeared down the next block. I hoped for recess and summer vacation. And I hoped for the streetlights to stay on longer at night to have more time to stay outside and catch fireflies.

In high school, I hoped for a certain boy to ask me to the dance, to make the cheerleading squad, and to pass algebra. (Math was never my thing.) I hoped to pass my driver's test and for my dad to trust me with the family car. In college, I hoped to get good grades and someday get married, become a mother, raise a family, find meaningful work and live a happy life.

Everything turned out more or less as I'd hoped, but not without my fair share of disappointments and challenges. But did any of these things happen because I hoped for them? Or did they happen because of something else? And what about the disappointments? Was all my hoping for naught? I'm left wondering, "What's hope got to do with it?"

If someone is drowning and you throw a lifeline called *hope*, do they have anything to cling to, or is it akin to handing them cotton candy? Will they experience a few happy moments before they drown, or will hope give them the will to stay afloat long enough to find a log to grab onto and make it back to shore?

If someone is diagnosed with a serious illness, does hope play a role in his recovery? If they receive a prognosis of six months left to live, should they surrender all hope of ever getting better and prepare to die, or will hope activate the healing process?

I used to think that hope was a sinking ship, and it was better not to climb on board. I viewed hope as a form of denial, an excuse for not taking action. One can *hope* things turn out but never take action to make it happen. I believed hope was the currency of the lazy or those who lacked courage.

But I've realized something about hope that has made me perceive it through a different lens. While hope alone is not enough to effect change, I believe it has a key role to play. Here's my case for hope:

For anyone who's ever felt like all was lost and the situation was hopeless, life appears bleak. In a state of hopelessness, one can see no light at the end of the tunnel. Hopelessness is a dark, dense energy that sucks the life out anyone who's ever been in that place. It is the energy of depression and despair. Not a place anyone ever wants to be, and yet millions of people reside in a state of hopelessness.

Sharon, age 72, is undergoing treatment for an aggressive form of breast cancer. Her journey has been a difficult one, challenging on every level. She had a difficult time tolerating the nine rounds of chemotherapy and wasn't sure if she could make it through. Every day is a struggle to live with the side effects that wrack her body.

She made it through chemo, and her tumors shrank enough for her doctor to perform a lumpectomy and removal of all the lymph nodes. The original diagnosis showed four nodes affected, but post-surgical lab analysis showed they didn't get all the cancer in the breast and three additional lymph nodes showed activity. So surgery #2 was necessary to remove the rest of the cancer from the breast and radiation treatments began soon thereafter.

Sharon is now halfway through her thirty radiation treatments. Her breast is so badly burned she developed a condition called cellulitis, a form of staph infection. Her doctor had to pause the radiation treatments long enough to treat her cellulitis, then right back to radiation. She is in enormous pain and discomfort and confessed she is suffering as much with radiation as she did with chemotherapy.

As Sharon looks ahead, all she can see is more suffering; fifteen more sessions of radiation, three weeks of healing from the aftermath, plus another nine months of Herceptin infusions every three weeks. Can hope help her get through this?

As we spoke on the phone, Sharon shared her sense of defeat and feelings of hopelessness. *"What is all this for?"* she asks. *"I feel so beaten down and alone, I don't know if I can make it through this."*

I reminded her she needed only to make it through today. That's all there is, in reality. Just today. Focus on today and the rest will take care of itself. Sharon took a deep breath and heaved a sigh of relief. *"Thank you,"* she said. *"I keep getting out in front of myself, which gets me into trouble."*

"Yes," I agreed. *"When we project ourselves too far into the future, the dark part of our minds can have a field-day and make up bad scenarios. Stay right here, at home in today. You can only live one day at a time anyway, so focus on here and now, just the next breath if that's as far as you can see."*

For the hopeless, hope can be a match struck in a dark tunnel, a moment of light, enough to show the path ahead and the way out. Hope is a flashbulb that lights up a room, revealing everything in it, and when the room goes black again, hope leaves an imprint in our memory of the hidden landscape. Hope gives a glimpse of possibility not seen in the darkness and shows the way, but for only an instant. We must act on hope or it becomes nothing more than a pleasant memory, a nice moment.

Hope is the mother of change. It is the womb of discontent from which change is born. Hope is the spark that lights the fire of inspiration and imagination. Hope ignites the flame, but we are the ones who must add fuel to the flames to keep the fire alive. Our commitment, passion and intention can transform that spark into a raging fire.

It takes enormous courage to be a human being in these times when everything is changing and little is certain. Being lost and stuck is part of the process of becoming found, so don't despair and don't give up hope. Know that you're developing the character qualities you're going to need when you come through this time. Sometimes, all it takes is just to focus on the next breath.

Food for Thought

- When in your life have you felt hopeless?

- What was/is happening when you felt this way?

- How long did you stay there?

- How did you go beyond?

- What did you learn from the experience?

CHAPTER TWELVE

What Would You Do If You Knew You Couldn't Fail?

Many years ago, I had an important dream. In it, I was on a tightrope high above the ground, wearing a business suit, carrying a briefcase, and wearing high heel shoes. I looked like a buttoned up corporate type. This couldn't be farther from how I normally appear in waking life. Let's just say the traditional female corporate suit has never found a place in my closet, and I gave up wearing anything higher than 1½ in. heels years ago. I've never owned a briefcase unless you count the case I carry my computer in. But nevertheless, there I was in the dream, all decked out like a foreigner.

As the dream unfolds, I'm watching myself from an enlightened observer's viewpoint, making my way along the tightrope, every muscle tensed. My concentration is like a laser beam, every step placed with precision. Falling would bring certain death. There is no room for failure. There is also no net.

At least not one I can see. But just beneath the tightrope, out of my view, for as far as the eye can see, are angel wings. The wings are so close they almost brush up against the tightrope. But I'm blinded by my fear of falling so I cannot see them.

My own observer voice in the dream whispers, *"Look how hard she's working to keep from falling. What a pity she doesn't know she's safe. Someone should tell her."*

I wake up and realize the dream's message: *"No matter how complicated and difficult the dances on the tightrope may appear, remember Love is always present. You cannot fall. Rest in this Love."*

The woman in the dream couldn't see and didn't know that a force greater than she had her back. She didn't know and couldn't see because she didn't trust that anyone or anything could ever have her back. She was so busy proving to herself and others that she was independent and capable and needed no one, that when Love *was* present, she missed it.

Oh, how I recognized this woman as myself! There I was, on the tightrope, proving to my mother that I didn't need a man to take care of me. I was all buttoned up and in control and I would show her and everyone that I could take care of myself. What I failed to see was the price I was paying for this *"I don't need anybody, I can take care of myself"* attitude.

What did it cost me? Well, let's start with my marriage to the father of my two daughters. I was unable to receive or accept his love even though in my heart of hearts, I now know he was in fact, the love of my life. I couldn't see and didn't get it at the time. I came to this realization towards the end of his life as we came back together after thirty years of being divorced and he was dealing with Alzheimer's. Perhaps this story is part of a different book. It was a long and difficult chapter in the life of my children, in his life and in my own. I missed the love of my life when it was right in front of me. I was not mature or worthy enough to receive this love.

So the dream showed me the price of not trusting or allowing Love. There were the angel wings just below my feet. Love was right there, always present, always with me. And I couldn't let it in. I still grieve for that woman I used to be. How closed and fearful she was! But I'll tell you this: I'm also proud of her because she woke up. She went through the pain of facing herself and her greatest fears and she broke through into joy, freedom and aliveness. She did the necessary inner work that allowed her to break through and finally come home to her Self. She came home to her authentic Self, the one in her who was never lost, the one in her who always knew who she was and why she was here. That's the woman who is writing this book, now, after all these years and all this pain. And I love her!

The power of this dream was realizing that the "I" I call "me", is not separate from this Love. This great, universal Love is always present. Love is who we are.

If anyone reading this can relate, I hope you can use my story to help you wake up. Please don't spend your life believing that you can't trust or allow love in your life. I'm here to tell you this is a mistake in your thinking. It's simply not true. I'm here to take you by the shoulders and gently shake you awake and urge you to come to home yourself. Let's find the path together.

I had an artist friend draw a picture of the dream so I could hold on to the image. I still keep it in my bedroom where I see it every day. It's a great reminder of this one eternal truth: Love Is.

How quickly this awareness gets lost as we take up the trek on the tightrope! We work so hard to keep from falling.

> *"Leap and the net will appear."*
> *Julia Cameron, The Artist's Way*

So what if you couldn't fail? What if that tightrope on which you're walking so carefully is only an inch above the ground? Or what if there really is a power greater than you that has your back if you trust and allow it?

What if the way life works is declaring an intention without any evidence that you can do it, and then leaping and the path becomes apparent? What have you got to lose, except your illusion of being safe and secure and perhaps a warm seat on the bench?

Like most humans, you most likely want to see the net before you leap. But what if the path ahead doesn't show itself until you've demonstrated a commitment and willingness to go for it, be uncomfortable, be inconvenienced, and like the Nike ad says, "Just do it"!

Let's face it: if the pull of your history is stronger than your commitment to manifest a different future, you'll stay where you are. So if you're telling yourself you want a different result and it's not happening, look to see if what you're committed to is being right about the story and keeping that bench warm.

Human beings are master storytellers. Life happens and we make up a story about it. It is our human nature to interpret life's events every moment. We're such masters at bringing meaning to each moment we don't even know we're doing it. The process is transparent to us. We do it instantaneously. Thus, we forget that we're the ones who are making up what the story means! We then proceed to live our lives as if our stories are the truth! We collapse what happens in our lives into the stories we tell ourselves about what happens.

This process is akin to baking a cake. You fold all the ingredients into the mix until you can no longer distinguish the flour from the sugar from the butter, from the eggs. Put it in the oven and bake it for 20-30 years or more (how long have you've been polishing up your story?) and the cake becomes an impenetrable rock. That's how our stories become our truths. Repeated long enough and often enough, we lose sight of the facts and are left with our perceptions, masquerading as facts.

Human beings are hard wired to make up meaning about everything in life. We rarely, if ever, view life's events as neutral events, which is what they actually are. If we're meaning-manufacturing machines, what's the alternative? If our nature is to interpret and fabricate meaning about everything, how do we *not* make up things? How can we know the truth?

Here's the bad news: You're always going to make up a story about what happens. That's the way it is with us humans.

Here's the good news: You can make up anything you want. So why not make up a story that empowers you to go forward? As the storyteller, you're the one who chooses the plot, the characters, the subplots, the action, etc. You can make it up however you want.

You might resist this idea ... but try this on for size. The truth is whatever you say it is. You're the one who invests your energy in being right about whatever you think is true. Why not be right about a choice that drives your life forward? Yes, you might fail. But life doesn't come with a money-back guarantee. You get a ticket to ride. That's it. People fall and skin their knees or even their hearts.

Not to be crass, but so what? Sometimes our biggest challenges are also our biggest teachers. So don't be afraid to learn. The only failure is to live your life in such a way that when you reach the end, you look back and are filled with regrets about never having gone for it.

I have leapt with no net in sight more times than I can count. Sometimes, the chasm has been so wide, I've been airborne for years! I've had lots of time during flight to second guess and rethink my decision to leap, but since I'd already gone for it, I needed to become creative and figure out how to land on my feet.

Sometimes I've stuck the landing like an Olympic gymnast. Other times, I've barely made the net, catching it with a hangnail. Still other times, I've missed the net on the first pass, hit the ground and bounced back up making the net on the second pass and still have the bruises to show for it! But I wouldn't trade those bruises for a tidy life lived on the sidelines.

Would you rather stay safe or risk being free? What would you do if you knew you couldn't fail? The choice is yours. Ask yourself, "Is my life how I want it to be?" If your answer is "Yes, I don't want to change a thing", bravo to you, and enjoy the ride. But if you've come to a place in the road and the path you're on is a dead end, if you feel you've outgrown your stories and they now only constrain you, it's time to explode those old stories, bring them to an end, and write a new one that opens the door to freedom. Time to prepare for the brave new life that awaits!

An Assignment

Write down all the stories you're ready to conclude. Put them in a fireproof bowl and set them on fire or put them through the shredder. This is literally an exploding assignment. Be prepared for your ego to jump up and down, wave its arms and warn you against doing this. The ego's job is to keep these stories alive and installed on the hard drive of your life. Explode them and you're robbing the ego of one of its major duties. You'll have to figure out some other job for it like, chopping wood, carrying water and making sure all the socks come out of the dryer.

After you've exploded the stories that have defined you and your box, leaned out, broken free and risen up, next leap. Leap because you must. Leap because it's who you are and it's why you came to the planet. Leap because it's what the world needs.

In leaping you have to pull out all the stops, throw off the shackles, align with your higher self, attune with your true nature, and say "yes". It will have you step off the cliff before you can see the net and create whatever is needed to get you to the other side. Maybe you'll end up inventing a whole new technology for how human beings can get from here to there.

Food for Thought
Leaping Assignment – The 100 Day Challenge

What would you do if you knew you couldn't fail? Want to find out?

Imagine giving yourself 100 days to manifest an important goal in your life. If your goal is too big to be achieved in 100 days, begin by taking the first big chunk out of it.

One hundred days of concentrated focus on an area of your life you want to improve is a powerful and effective way to bring about lasting change.

"The journey of 1000 miles begins with a single step."

Lao Tzu

How many single steps can you take in 100 days? What areas of your life are up for review?

Pick a focus for the next 100 days. You can start today. Select one (or more) area(s) to concentrate on for the next 100 days, but keep it simple. You'll be amazed at your ability to get things done when you concentrate your energy by zeroing in on what's most important.

Remember to make S.M.A.R.T. goals: Specific, Measurable, Attainable, Realistic and Timely. How many and by when? Here are examples of the kinds of goals you might set:

Health - If you're facing current health challenges, how will you care for yourself? Who can you ask for support? Lose how many pounds in 100 days? Exercise how many times per week? Clean up your diet? (Ex. cut out dairy, wheat, sugar, meat), Stop smoking? Reduce or eliminate your "adult beverage" intake? Spend time in the outdoors appreciating Mother Nature at least once a week?

Finances - Is it time to get your financial act together? Do a realistic inventory of inflows and outflows. Do you live within your means? If not, set up a budget and follow it. Structure helps. Trim the fat from the outflow (do you need all those premium channels?) Dine out less. Pay down, or if you can, pay off credit card debt. How will you bring the outflow into alignment with the inflow? How can you increase the inflow? Change careers? Negotiate for a raise in your current job?

Career Development - Are you unemployed? Underemployed? Do you need to downsize your business? Consider the following suggestions:

Update your resume and send out how many/day? Schedule how many job interviews per week? How can you make yourself indispensable at your present job? How can you add value to your company or organization? What skills need to be updated or developed?

Relationships - With job insecurity so prevalent, it's easy to lose sight of our needs for relatedness. Yet without the important people in our lives, nothing else matters. Who's most important in your life? How much time do you spend with them or communicate with them? It might be time to schedule a visit back home, spend quality time with Mom and Dad. Plan a family reunion and take the lead in organizing it. Commit to spending quality time each week with your spouse and children.

Community - Life works better when we focus beyond our personal needs. Where, how and with whom can you make a difference in your community? What volunteer opportunities call to you? How many hours per week can you devote to contributing and with whom?

Recreation - All work and no play makes Jack and Jill dull robots. Make time for fun! Focus is important and hard work is necessary, now more than ever. But we also need time to relax and enjoy the ride; otherwise, you might get to your goal and be too worn out to appreciate what you accomplished.

What activities will you schedule for a "time out for play"? Will you take a weekend trip? Go camping with the family? Attend a silent retreat or workshop? Go to a movie and out to dinner with friends? Take a salsa class?

Personal Growth - Are you a life-long learner? Self-development is as important as everything else on this list. How will you open yourself to new learning? Attend a seminar? Take a painting class? Join a book club?

The Inner Life - All that activity in the outer world needs to be balanced by spending time in the inner realm. How will you create inner and outer balance? Cultivate a meditation practice and commit to spending time in meditation each day? Attend the church of your choice each week? Practice yoga? Attend a silent retreat? Write in your journal?

What will you commit to for the next 100 days that will help you get unstuck and moving forward?

Four Tips to Help You Stay Oon Track

1. **Get a buddy** - you don't have to be the lone ranger. Synergy is a powerful dynamic. You're in this together. Schedule check-in times to be accountable to each other.

2. **Work with a coach** a coach is trained to help you identify and get past the obstacles that pop up along the way and will hold you accountable. If it's not in your budget, all the more reason to have a good buddy system in place.

3. **Keep a journal -** the journey of going for your goals is as important as reaching them. The process is where the learning is. Record your thoughts, feelings, and experiences along the way. Look back in 100 days and see how far you've come.

4. **Enjoy the ride** - it need not be the arduous trek up the Himalayas. It's the journey of your life unfolding day by day for 100 days at a time. Have fun!

Take stock of where you are at the end of that time and give yourself a reward when you finish. You made it through another 100 days of living! Isn't that reason enough to pop the bubbly?

Here's the thing, you will live your life for the next 100 days anyway. Why not be up to something that wouldn't happen by default? Why not live those 100 days as if they were the last 100 days of your life? Who knows? You might even be up for another 100 days after that!

CHAPTER THIRTEEN

Failure: The Other "F" Word

"Failure sucks, but instructs."

Robert Sutton, Professor of Management Sciences and Engineering, Stanford University.

In the previous chapter, I asked you to consider what you'd do if you knew you couldn't fail? But what if you do fail? Shouldn't we learn something about failure so we can make the most of it? What if we could transform our relationship with failure so it didn't stop us, but instead inspired us?

What if you knew what you wanted to do with your life and thought you knew how to get there. What if you went for it and you failed? You thought you gave it everything, but still, it didn't happen. At times like these, it's tempting to lose faith and give up. But is that the only option?

Most business schools teach their entrepreneur majors that failure is a necessary part of learning and innovation. Their motto is: *"Fail early, fail fast, fail cheap."*

Sounds like this advice could also apply to the rest of us. In other words, when failure arrives at your doorstep, don't turn it away, rather invite it in. I know, it might sound crazy, but perk up your ears and get this.

Failure comes with some goodies that are necessary steps on your way to success, so you'd better get to know this part of the process early on. Learn to make friends with your failed efforts as much as the ones that worked. You might just learn more from failure than from success.

If you haven't attended an entrepreneur program in business school, chances are you haven't been encouraged to fail, much less taught to celebrate your failures. But listen to this: every year during Entrepreneur Week, Stanford's Technology Ventures Program gives an award to the "Biggest Failure" in their Entrepreneurship Tournament.

Imagine that! Failures can be celebrated! Let that sink in for a minute. What could be possible if you applied that philosophy to your own life, and specifically, when it comes to manifesting your dreams?

Very few things in life are clear-cut and straightforward. Manifesting your dreams, maybe even the ones that seem impossible to achieve, qualifies as one of those endeavors that often seems to take you to places you never imagined and weren't part of the original plan. Life might have a different path in store for you than the one you had in mind.

Consider the story of Nathan. Nathan grew up in a small town in New England, the son of a minister. But this life wasn't for him. He always knew he wanted to be an actor.

Inspired by actor Mark Ruffalo *and with no training or experience*, Nathan went to an open casting call, auditioned and landed the part. He moved to LA and worked off and on for a while in Hollywood, but things didn't go as he'd hoped.

Discouraged, he was set to leave Hollywood when, "out of the blue", Nathan met a big music producer and spent the next four years as a professional drummer (another passion of his) for bands like the

Dixie Chicks and Christina Aguilera. He hadn't played drums since he was a kid! He was living a life that was not part of his plan, but he had steady work.

Still, in his heart, Nathan couldn't shake his desire to be an actor. Even with the buzz around the music industry, he felt his life had gotten off course and he was missing his own boat. He spent some time "in a dark period" not knowing what to do next.

Then, another "out of the blue" thing happens; a call from his old manager, with whom he hadn't spoken in five years, invites him to audition for a film directed by Mark Ruffalo and he gets the part! He got to work with his favorite actor, the one who inspired him to go into acting in the first place.

In his own words, here's where Nathan finds himself now: *"And here I sit now in total flux and still pretty much broke, and a little frightened, with NO jobs presently on the horizon, pondering daily what comes next. Life has been proving to me, however, that around every unseen turn lies an even greater adventure than the last if you're willing to take the ride. But sometimes it's really hard not to panic. Even with all this evidence in my own life I'm still sitting here trying not to panic."*

Nathan's work is to keep the faith and keep breathing. And to know that greater things are on their way. He could use this time in the void productively. Maybe it's now his turn to make a difference for someone coming along with a dream, just like his.

Wouldn't it be nice if everything you ever wanted went according to plan, no surprises or delays, no unexpected challenges to throw you off course? Not according to Robert Komisar , a partner in KPCB venture capital firm. *"The ones who go through life failing little or not at all are not as wise as those who have actually failed,"* says Komisar.

The word "failure" carries a heavy charge in most cultures. No one volunteers for failure. It seems to come, when it does, either in spite of the best-laid plans or because those plans weren't actually as well laid out as you thought. But it always comes bearing a gift.

There is much to be learned from failure, so it's a good idea to get on top of it, sooner rather than later. You were meant to do great things, including learning from what you did that didn't work. To do that means looking at failure through a different lens.

Failure, or breakdown, is life's way of calling a "Time out". It's the referee blowing the whistle. So stop doing what didn't work. Don't spend time in self-recrimination or look for someone else to blame.

Do an inquiry. Breakdown only occurs in the context of commitment. No commitment, no breakdown. Look to discover what commitment had you take the action that produced a different result than the one you wanted.

Be honest with yourself. Look to see, inside this commitment, what action(s) didn't work. This is not the time to go into denial or pretend you don't know. Even if you think you don't know, ask yourself, "If I did know, what would it be?"

Once you see what didn't work, ask yourself, "What was missing in me that made me get off course?" Maybe you weren't sufficiently focused, or lacked self-confidence. We're trying to find how you can realign yourself to get back on track with your original commitment.

Reevaluate your commitment and recommit. Are you still committed to this dream? Is this what you really want? If so, recommit. You can expect that life will test you to make sure you're really committed. If your answer is "yes", then re-focus your commitment and go again.

Food for Thought

- Bring to mind your biggest failure. In a few words, write down what happened.

- What did you learn about yourself through this failure?

- Where do you stop yourself?

- What limiting beliefs dominate your thinking and choices?

- To what fears do you give up your power?

CHAPTER FOURTEEN

Commitment: The Other "C" Word

"Consider a breakfast of ham and eggs.
The pig is committed. The chicken is involved."

Anonymous

Think of the pig in the above scenario and you'll know what we mean by being committed. What are you so committed to in your life that you'll do whatever it takes to make it happen? Or to put it another way, are you committed to your commitments?

During a seminar I led with a group of students in Taipei, as part of the experience, people were asked to make certain commitments, or give their agreement to a set of ground rules. One of the rules was to be on time for each session.

It's common for people to give their word and then not give it another thought. For a moment, they make a conscious choice to play by the rules, but oftentimes, they go right back to their automatic behaviors. If someone is habitually late, it's almost guaranteed they'll break that agreement.

So it was not surprising that one of the students was late to the session on the final day. One of the training staff members called to check in on the student and was informed he had been involved in a motorcycle accident, he was all right and he would be coming, although late.

Eddie arrived 40 minutes later. When he walked into the room, his hands and arms were bandaged, his clothes were bloody and torn. And he had a huge smile on his face! He proceeded to tell us that the police wanted to take him to the hospital for treatment, but he refused. He told them, *"I can deal with this on my own. I have to be at the training. I'm already late. I promised to be on time."* They tried to persuade him to come to the police department to fill out some paperwork but Eddie deferred: *"I'll be back tomorrow and take care of it. Please let me go now, because I need to get to the training."*

I would have been perfectly understanding had Eddie chosen not to return because of his accident or came in even later because he'd gone to the hospital to have his wounds treated. This would seem like the sensible thing to do!

But not for Eddie. He was committed to his commitment to be on time and even though he broke that commitment, he was not going to use his accident as an excuse to derail his experience, and not come back. Eddie came back, took responsibility for being late, didn't play the victim and finished the training. This is commitment! Doing whatever it takes.

Let's consider the Six Levels of Commitment:

1. I'm 100% committed. Whatever it takes.

2. I'm committed – unless …

3. It sounds like a good idea. Let's talk about it.

4. I want to, but …

5. I wish, I hope it happens.

6. I don't care if it happens.

"Do whatever it takes" has a caveat in my book: "As long as it does not do physical harm to yourself or another". There are ways to keep your commitments without endangering yourself or anyone else and I highly recommend you make those choices instead of ones that put you at risk of physical harm.

When you're operating at 100% commitment you'll be required to get outside your comfort zone, take risks, and make choices you haven't been willing to make up until now.

Or maybe you're someone who has always settled for 99%. You commit to a goal or go for a dream and you make it 99% of the way there. But something has you stop at that point and not cross the finish line.

There are numerous reasons why we do this. Can you think of yours? Which one of these excuses do you give yourself?

1. This is good enough. There's such a small difference, it doesn't matter if I cross the finish line or not. It's no big deal.

2. I'm afraid to go the last mile. What if I don't make it?

3. I always fail. I always find a way to sabotage myself right at the end.

4. What if I succeed? That sounds scary too!

5. I've never finished anything I start.

Maybe you have other stories you tell yourself about why you don't go the full 100%. Here's the thing: you either have the result you say you want or you have a good reason for why you don't have the result. Reasons or results? Which do you settle for?

What does this have to do with being sucked into the turbulence of these times and losing your way? Think about it. If you spend your whole life never getting to the finish line, and settling instead for reasons about why you don't finish, you're living in a fantasy. What's another name for fantasy? Non-reality. What's another name for non-reality? Lost!

What we see on the Levels of Commitment chart, from 2-6, is room for excuses.

#2 - I'm committed unless ... unless what? It rains? You stub your toe?

#3 - Sounds like a good idea. Let's talk about it. How long have you been talking about a good idea, but never taken any action on it? You know the saying, "talk is cheap." Stop talking and start taking action.

#4 - I want to, but ... Seriously? But what? Your boss won't let you? Your husband/wife/mother/father/significant other will be uncomfortable if you do? How long have you been "wanting" this result? Did "wanting" have you take action? "Wanting" something, but taking no action to create it, makes for a good story and others might give you credit for "wanting". But this is not commitment.

#5 - I wish, I hope it happens – Recall, I've already made my case for hope. Wishing is in the same category as hoping. Wish and hope all you want. Until you couple it with action you'll be recycling that wish again and again in the "stuck" department of your life. No commitment here.

#6 - I don't care – At least this is honest. Game over.

If your commitment is at 100%, and you've lost your way, it's your commitment that will dig you out of the hole, clear the fog and get you headed in the right direction. It's your commitment that will override your fear of humiliation or looking foolish, or afraid of what others will think or say and get you moving towards found. It's your 100%

commitment that will get you out of bed in the morning when your tired self urges you to hit the snooze button and stay in bed just a bit longer.

It's your 100% commitment that will have you leap when no net is in sight. It will have you choose the thing your fear tells you not to do. It'll have you override the voices that say you don't have the background, experience, qualifications, contacts, money, time, energy or expertise to be taking this thing on. But you'll do it anyway, and figure it out on the way across the chasm.

This is the blessing and the curse of being 100% committed to going for your dreams. When you reach this level, you are unstoppable. Not everyone is going to like or agree with your choices, so get used to it. Become the source of your own approval because there's nobody else out there to fill you up at this level. It's all you. This is the "grit" you'll need to get back on track and get moving.

Food for Thought

- From what level of commitment 1-6, are you operating?

- What excuses do you give yourself for being less than 100% committed?

- What are you settling for instead?

- What limiting belief would you need to give up to get to 100%?

CHAPTER FIFTEEN

Beyond the Box: Dare to Dream Big

"Dreams are the answers to questions that
we haven't yet figured out how to ask."

Fox Mulder

Once you've gone beyond the box, once you've leaned out, broken free and have risen up, then what? Where do you go in this brave new world? I suggest you turn to your dreams. They've been calling to you, been waiting for you to get past playing small. It's time to dream big, and once you've caught fire with a big dream, let that dream call you forth to play big.

"Don't be pushed by your problems. Be led by your dreams."

So think about this: what are those dreams you dare not to dream? You know, the ones so big and overwhelming, so scary and seemingly impossible, you can't even begin to wrap your mind around them? I'm talking about the kind of dreams that make your toes curl and your stomach churn and make you ask yourself, *"Who do you think you are to have such a dream?"*

Good question! But how about this: "Who do you think you're not?"

What's the story you tell yourself about why your dream is impossible? *It really doesn't matter, I don't really want this, why bother, it's too late, I've already missed it, nobody would believe in me, who do I think I am, it's just an illusion, a pipe dream, a fantasy, nobody in their right mind would ever do this, I'm deluding myself, this is stupid, I'm wasting my time, I don't have what it takes, I'm too old, too young, don't know what I'm doing, don't have the money, the time, the education* or *experience, I don't have enough self-discipline, I'm not worthy or deserving, I might fail so why bother, I might succeed and then what?*

These are not empowering conversations. They limit your creativity and kill your courage. It's much more empowering to have a dream that calls you forth, something to move towards rather than away from.

Many younger people tell me they don't have any dreams, or they haven't found any yet. They don't even know where to look. Others say they used to have dreams, but that was long ago, *before life got in the way.*

So, let's begin exploring: **where do you look to find your dreams?**

The answer to that question lays inside the answer to another important question:

What makes a life worth living?

This question drills down several layers beneath external conditions and puts the inquiry smack dab in the middle of a gold mine. It invites you to enter the realm of what lives in your heart of hearts and soul of souls.

There, more questions arise. The truth is, the gold to be mined lies in the questions themselves.

I love this Rilke quote: *"Have patience with everything that remains unsolved in your heart. Try to love the questions themselves, like locked rooms and like books written in a foreign language."*

Is it just about surviving, making it through? Are we born with a destiny to fulfill or do we come to life as a blank slate? Does fate play a role in how our lives turn out or do we create them out of the choices we make?

From these questions, others arise:

Is an acorn *destined* to become an oak tree?

Is a caterpillar *destined* to become a butterfly?

When I think about my own life and who I've become, I can see that even as a kid, I was always curious to know about other people and what made them who they are. My career as a teacher, trainer, coach, therapist, and public speaker began in my parents' garage when I was 7 years old. I used to borrow folding chairs from a neighbor, line them up in neat little rows and invite the kids in the neighborhood to come over and "share". I stood in front of the room and encouraged the kids to share about kid stuff, summer vacation activity, scouting, dancing lessons and the like. Even then, I wanted to get inside people's stories!

Decades later, I'm still at it, still enlivened by my work with people, and still compelled to explore the elegant mysteries of our human existence.

The Acorn Theory

In his book, *The Soul's Code*, Dr. James Hillman, founder of archetypal psychology, asserts, *"Each person enters the world 'called', like an oak tree, to fulfill their soul's agenda."*

"When all the souls had chosen their lives, they went before Lachesis. And she sent with each as the guardian of his life and the fulfiller of his choice, the daimon that he had chosen."

Plato, Republic Book X

Hillman suggests every human being is born with a defining image, that our soul's agenda is encoded in us before we are even born and that we come into human form to carry out that agenda.

"Fate, providence and destiny *play significant roles in determining the main plot of our lives"*, says Hillman. He warns that today, the awareness of coming with a "calling" is lost amidst the din of modern life and in the process, *"the essential mystery at the heart of each human life"* gets ignored.

What if your destiny was encoded in the DNA of your soul before you were born? And what if your big dreams are the natural unfolding of that destiny, wanting to be lived through you?

What if all the upsets and breakdowns of your life, all the seeming detours and backtracking were essential and necessary parts of your process, all intended to prepare you to fulfill your destiny?

With the pressing needs of life in these times, it's easy to lose sight of what inspires or calls us. It seems to require all of one's energy to just get through the "ordinary" demands of life. Who has the luxury of time and the resources to go for their big dreams?

And yet, without a dream that calls to you, life becomes flat and robotic. It's not getting through the mechanics of life that makes it worth living.

What makes life worth living is the sense that a unique purpose awaits you. What if your dream is waiting for you to discover it, claim it, grow it, and live it?

The Story of Philippe Petit- Man On Wire!

This is the story of one man's impossible dream. He did something no one in the world had ever done before or will ever do again. *It's literally impossible!*

Philippe Petit is a French *"wire walker"*. As a young boy, Petit dreamed of dancing on a high wire, but settled for a rope strung between two trees instead.

He spent his much of his adult life as a street performer, and spent hot summer days performing on the streets of Paris, juggling balls and fruit, while riding a unicycle. But this was child's play for him. His sights were set much higher. Literally.

Petit was a bit of a rascal, to put it mildly. To live his passion required that he take his street performances to the farthest edges he could imagine and he almost always ended up being arrested at the end of each act, for what he did was clearly outside the law.

One day, while visiting his dentist because of a toothache, he picked up a magazine in the waiting room and read a story that would fire his imagination and take him to a place no human being has been before or will be again. He began to dream a dream that looked completely impossible, which to his way of thinking meant, *"Go for it"*. So he made a plan and set to work.

After many years of dreaming, planning and false starts, on August 7, 1974, Petit, together with his team of co-conspirators, managed to rig a wire between the Twin Towers of the World Trade Center and spent 45 minutes dancing on it, before the police threatened to pluck him off it with a helicopter and he chose to come off on his own.

His amazing story is the subject of the 2008 documentary *Man On Wire*! It won the 2009 Academy Award for Best Documentary. In accepting the award, the director, James Marsh, told the audience, *"Nothing is impossible"*. Then Petit, in typical fashion, bounded up on stage and gave the shortest acceptance speech in Oscar history: *"It just doesn't get much better than this!"*

The man who danced between the Twin Towers now can only dream of what he did, for the towers existed only as an architect's drawings when he caught the dream, and now they no longer stand, having been completely destroyed in the terrorist attacks on September 11, 2001.

He didn't know it at the time, but Philippe's dream had an expiration date. And perhaps yours does too. For, if we wait too long to manifest our dreams, they can die inside us. Our songs may go unsung, our gifts ungiven. Isn't it time you got to work, creating your dreams?

Where to begin?

Look to your childhood for clues. What were the things you did because they were natural to do, or that in fact, maybe you couldn't do otherwise?

Consider the story of Sarah Hughes, who at sixteen won the gold medal in women's figure skating at the 2002 Olympics in Salt Lake City. Sarah began skating at the age of three. When she was five, her father took a home movie of her and asked: *"What do you want to be when you grow up?"* The adorable five-year old did not miss a beat when she responded, **"I can't wait to win the gold medal at the Olympics"**.

Did you hear that? She didn't say, *"I hope I win the gold medal"*, she said, *"I can't wait to win the gold medal"*. **It was already a done deal.** She already had herself standing on the podium, singing the national anthem. And she was five! It took eleven more years to bring her dream into form. Eleven years of hard work and sacrifice. Eleven years of devotion and commitment.

As the underdog behind teammates Michelle Kwan and Sasha Cohen, and the Russian, Irina Slutskaya, Hughes pulled off the upset of a lifetime. Going into the final skate in fourth place after the short program, and skating second in rotation, Sarah had nothing to lose. She went out and set the ice on fire, skating one of the most technically difficult programs in Olympic history, landing seven triple jumps, including two triple/ triple combinations!

Sarah the underdog, ended up winning the gold, electrifying the world with her magical performance. When interviewed afterwards, she remarked: *"When I started my program ... there was a big clock in the corner and I looked and it said nine o'clock exactly. And it was funny, because when I was standing on the podium, it said exactly 10 p.m., and* **this whole hour had changed my life***."*

Sarah skated to win. Michelle Kwan skated not to lose.

How about you? How are you "skating" your life?

Look to what matters to you, look to what you love, look to what flows out of you like honey. There, you'll find the spark of imagination to fan into your impossible dream. Then trust it, and follow it.

Here are some tangible actions to support you finding your big dream:

Map Your Way to Your Dreams

In workshops I lead on this topic, I have participants make a Dream Map. You need a piece of poster board, some magazines to cut up, scissors, glue and some crayons or colored marking pens. Then have fun finding pictures that represent your dream and make a collage.

This is an intuitive process, so take your time. Let the images speak to you. Let them guide you where to place them on the paper. Use crayons or colored marking pens to write on your map and draw lines that connect each image.

A map to your dream will materialize right before your eyes! Place it where you'll see it every day. You'll be attracting the energies that align with your dream, so be prepared for new possibilities to open and be ready to take action on them.

If you think this is just child's play, think again! There's a principle at work here: *consciousness aligns with itself.* So while at the surface, it looks like you're just cutting out pictures from magazines and arranging them artfully on a piece of poster board, there's something "else" going on at the same time. This is an intuitive process that is like taking your right brain to the gym!

If you don't appreciate the importance of giving your right brain a creative workout, listen to this: Daniel Pink in his book *A Whole New Mind* says: *"Right brainers will rule the future,"* and *New York Times* columnist Thomas L. Friedman says in his books *The World Is Flat* and *Hot, Flat, and Crowded* that right brain activities are essential to jobs that cannot be outsourced. Friedman asserts: *"Creativity can be applied not only to creating art, but also to solving pressing problems of the day: finding sustainable energy solutions, developing innovative business ideas, and creating jobs".*

Here's what a workshop participant shared about her experience AFTER she made her map:

"First I have to say ideas and direction opened up. Once I had the "map" in front of me I began to know which way to go and I was able to get to work. That was one of my biggest problems before. I have heard it a million times, at seminars, in books, in conversations ... Put your plan down on paper, make it real. I never did it. Making the dream map gave me something tangible and as a result I was able to make decisions about what to do first instead of just THINKING about the plan. I was able to begin DOING something. And when I look at it ... it makes me smile."

So go ahead! Give your right brain a creative workout and have fun mapping your way to your dreams. Once you've created your map choose an object that represents your dream and makes it tangible.

Food for Thought – Manifesting Your Impossible Dream

Zero in on the one, big dream that speaks the loudest to you.

Chances are, this is the umbrella dream that makes all the others possible. Maybe you want to create an intimate, romantic, lasting relationship that includes marriage and children. Maybe you want to start and build a business that utilizes your creativity and leadership capacities that also generates financial abundance and creates a positive impact for others. Maybe you want to take your health and fitness to a new level, your spiritual or personal development to a new level. Maybe your dream is to write that book you've been wanting to write all your life, get published, turn it into a best seller. Maybe your dream is about taking your gifts into the world in a bigger, more impactful way, becoming an influencer.

Make it tangible.

Once you've zeroed in on your big, seemingly impossible dream, find or create something tangible that represents your dream. It should be something that evokes the dream in your body, mind and spirit and calls forth your passion. It might be a photo, or a page torn from a magazine, like Philippe Petit did at the dentist's office. It could be a small statue or object.

Create a sacred space and place your object there with the intention of incubating your dream.

It might be the top of a bookcase, a shelf or the top of a dresser. Find a beautiful cloth to place there and add candles, photos, statues, flowers; whatever brings you back to your dream vision and fires your imagination.

Carrying a dream is like being pregnant. Dreams take time to unfold and manifest in form. Think of this sacred space as a womb for your dream, a place to do the inner work required to flesh it out.

Consider that incubating and giving birth to your dreams is holy work. It's what your soul came to do. For all that might seem impractical and improbable, there is also a certain inevitability to your dreams. Sooner or later, the soul will have its way with you.

So follow your bliss and while you're at it bring intention around incubating your dream. Build it and they will come. Hold it near and dear, nurture it, listen to it, let it guide you. Offer up a blessing to yourself and to the daimon that brought it to you. Maybe all you have for evidence is a spark of imagination or a burning passion you can't extinguish. Listen to this and follow it. It'll take you on an amazing adventure.

Declare your dream to a community of kindred spirits who will say "yes" and will support you finding the path.

Join a mastermind group or gather together a group of people, all of whom are committed to going for their own big dreams and supporting you in creating yours.

Don't be attached to how you get there.

Philippe and his co-hort, Jim Moore, were stopped by the security guard at the elevators on their first attempt to get to the top of the tower. *So they decided to walk to the top. 110 floors!* There's more than one way to get from A -Z, or even A-B, so don't get stuck on the mechanism. Chances are, you'll have to reinvent the path 100 times. Or 101.

Be willing to do whatever it takes.

Impossible is only a word. It's not a fact. Re-interpret what it means. Remember, Petit began by acknowledging that his dream was surely impossible. Then he said, *"OK, let's get to work."* And he did. Keep in mind, however, that "doing whatever it takes" could have adverse consequences if you don't stay smart. So be smart and don't compromise your integrity or inflict harm on others. It's about being 100% committed to your dream. Close all your back doors.

127

Take one small step every day that moves you in the direction of your dream.

Lao Tzu said, *"The journey of a thousand miles begins with a single step."* The first step is usually the hardest, so start now. What single step will you take today? You don't need to leap tall buildings in a single bound.

Eat a banana.

I know, it sounds crazy. That's the point! Acknowledge your fear, then give it a job to keep it busy and out of your way. Like eating a banana. No kidding! Concert pianists swear by them as a way to manage stage fright. The potassium serves as a beta blocker which soothes jangled nerves. Try it!

Hold on to your dream, be patient, and keep going.

OK there's actually three here, but who's counting? You have no idea what the time line is for the unfolding of your dream. You may think it's supposed to happen yesterday. The dream may have other ideas. Keep going for it anyway. Philippe Petit spent years planning his dream before the towers were even built.

Victory is sweet! Celebrate and share the glory.

We usually don't get to our dreams alone. This may turn out to be a relay race, a team effort. Share the glory with those who empower you along the way. Petit had an entire team who supported him. Without them, he couldn't have done it. *Everyone wins when one of us wins.* Who's on your "dream team"? If you're really smart, you'll enroll some key people to support you.

Cultivate a grateful heart.

Imagine your dream already fulfilled and give thanks ahead of time for its completion. Gratitude is the key to picking the locks that stand between you and your dreams. It focuses your energy like a laser beam. The universe rewards a grateful heart with even more abundance.

Get started now.

So it's your turn now. Time to get started. This isn't about just talking about your dreams. This is about taking action to manifest them. How about giving wings to your dreams and letting *them* fly?

Now, more than ever, consider giving yourself permission to resurrect your dreams and go for them. I don't mean you should go get stupid, but I do mean it's time to begin listening to the still, small voice within that's been telling you *"there's more to life than playing the game the way you've always played it."*

Our intention is to discover, claim, grow and express those dreams and **live them out loud**. What if everyone was busy living their impossible dreams and empowering and inspiring others?

CHAPTER SIXTEEN

The Gift of Gratitude

I t might sound counterintuitive, but when you've just leaned out, broken free and risen up, and you are standing in the rubble of your old box, in spite of all that appears to be scary and threatening, consider the possibility that this too, is a gift. I suggest to you that it is. When you've sorted through the rubble, be prepared to find something greater than you ever thought possible.

Even if you can't see your way right now and every step seems like it's headed towards the abyss, instead of cursing your fate and being a victim, what if instead, you reversed your thinking and viewed your circumstances as serving a purpose that perhaps you haven't figured out yet?

Consider the possibility that your current circumstances, no matter how frustrating or confounding, are there for your learning and to help you develop certain character muscles. To get to where your life is ordained to go, you must pass through these experiences along the way to gain the learning they present.

If we view life's events through the lens of seeing this as a learning opportunity, we're more likely to notice available possibilities that empower us to move forward. If we view life through the lens of "why did this happen?" we dig ourselves in even deeper.

So the most powerful way to mine the lessons from any experience is to begin by framing them as a gift instead of a tragedy. From this perspective, being grateful for what is happening can help you see beyond the pain in life's upsets to the gifts in those experiences.

If, instead of resisting what happens, you opened and allowed yourself to appreciate what life has put on your doorstep, can you see this attitude is more likely to bring you access to new solutions, new ways out, over and through the obstacles you appear to be facing?

Say one day you hear a knock at the door and you open it to discover someone has laid a bag of cow manure on your doorstep. Imagine your response! *"Who did this? Who put this here? This is terrible! What am I supposed to do with this manure?"*

Or imagine this response: *"Cow manure! How wonderful! Just what I need to fertilize my garden!"*

The truth is, life delivers "cow manure" disguised as learning opportunities all the time. If we're open to finding the hidden "gifts" in what life brings our way, and view them as learning opportunities, we'll be able to utilize them to find creative solutions to the challenges we face.

So let's consider gratitude as an essential tool for finding your way when you get lost on the journey, or when you're too confused to even get started. Or you've taken a wrong turn and come to a dead end.

Experts who study the art of happiness, health and overall life mastery, place gratitude as one of the highest emotional states possible and a strong medicine, a state of mind that releases endorphins, serotonin and helps combat the stress of uncertainty.

Behavioral experts believe that gratitude can alter the body's biochemistry, easing the flow of adrenaline in our system so that the body can become aligned and find balance. In a study of organ recipients, researchers from UC Davis and the Mississippi University for Women found that patients who kept "gratitude journals" scored better on measures of mental health, general health and vitality than those who kept only routine notes about their days.

Likewise, Drs. Michael McCullough and Robert Emmons, of Southern Methodist University and UC Davis, who conducted the Research Project on Gratitude and Thanksgiving, found similar results: daily gratitude exercises resulted in increased levels of alertness, enthusiasm, determination, optimism and energy. Their findings show that people who are grateful are also more likely to feel loved and express reciprocal kindness, since one act of gratitude encourages another.

Start right where you are by observing your world and your life and name the things in front of you for which you're grateful. You might not notice them at first if you've spent a lot of time being lost, feeling self-pity, anxiety, and depression. If your range of vision has shortened and narrowed because you haven't picked your head up, go ahead! Start now.

Every morning when I go out for my walk, I begin with noting what I'm grateful for right in front of me. My neighbor's garden, the sound of the birds singing, the fact I'm out walking, that I still have the strength and endurance to take these morning walks. I bring my focus from the things in the outer world for which I'm grateful to the things about myself I appreciate. For me, this is difficult to do, so it's a special assignment. Maybe it will be for you too.

I am reminded of my trip to India in 1996. I was there with a group of "pilgrims", a distinction made to us that trip by Marianne Williamson, who accompanied us. She reminded us we were not "tourists", but "pilgrims". This shift in context made something clear I hadn't understood before. To be on a "pilgrimage" is to travel to holy lands, to see through the eyes of holiness and, thus all that is seen becomes sacred.

Without the lens of my Western filters which saw suffering, I could experience the people and witness their beauty, even as some begged for money, most had little food and lived in mud homes. They brought us into their homes; we sat on rugs on top of dirt floors and shared what little food they had, prepared using dried oxen dung for cooking fuel. What I originally saw as suffering turned to beauty.

I knew during that experience it was a "blessing" moment, one I would remember for the rest of my life. Although we shared neither culture nor language, we shared the one language human beings have in common: the language of the heart. With such generosity, even the words "thank you" seemed inadequate. At that moment, I knew I wanted the rest of my life to be a pilgrimage. And so it is.

Imagine a world in which everyone in it cultivated gratitude for themselves, their lives and everything around them. How could that not produce more love? How could that not produce more peace and joy? If everyone is in "I am grateful", how could we not experience our own greatness reflected back by everyone around us?

We'd realize that we're not greater than anyone else. We'd understand that everyone has this greatness within himself or herself. By owning our greatness we can be a nudge for others to take up residency in theirs.

Food for Thought

Consider these daily gratitude practices:

- Begin and end your day with a gratitude prayer and a clear intention of being more grateful. Say "thank you" to the present moment throughout your day.

- Practice present-moment awareness. Be here now.

- Write "thank you" notes to friends, family members or co-workers just because.

- Do at least one random act of kindness for a stranger each day. Have fun with this!

- Keep a gratitude journal. List ten (or more) things you're grateful for in your journal each day – focus on people, situations or events.

- Practice "beauty appreciation". While on a walk or driving, look for the surrounding beauty. Allow yourself to absorb and connect with that beauty.

- Establish a daily prayer and/or meditation practice.

CHAPTER SEVENTEEN

What Makes a Life Worth Living?

"We must let go of the life we have planned,
so as to accept the one that is waiting for us."

Joseph Campbell

Consider that we're all going to die one day. The fact of our death
is ordained at the moment of our first breath. Yet human beings
live in denial of this truth. The unexpected death of a loved one
or the diagnosis of a life-threatening illness smacks us in the face, tears
away our denial, and forces us to look into the abyss of our own mortality.

After receiving a breast cancer diagnosis several years ago, I looked into
that abyss and feel fortunate to be free of cancer, living my life with
passion and purpose. Cancer both taught and blessed me.

Death, like it or not, is a given. Life is not. Life is a creative possibility we
shape and mold according to the choices we make during our time here
on earth. Given we know how the story ends, how do we make the time
we spend here worthy of this precious life we've been given?

Within each of us, there is an innate call to connect to the greater whole in our own, unique way. We're called to actualize our potential, discover and develop our gifts and contribute them to make a difference in the human condition. Each of us is called to be in service to life in a way that only we can fulfill. There is no one else who has the same combination of gifts or talents as you. You're one of a kind. Given your life is yours to create, what kind of life do you want to live?

Back in that first seminar experience that changed my life and set me on a new course, I knew I was not living in alignment with my higher purpose, yet I didn't know what that purpose was. The most difficult thing I've ever done was to leave that life in search of my authentic self and the life I was meant to live. That search took me far and wide, up and down. I was lost and stuck for the better part of twenty years. When I finally found myself, I found out who I am and why I'm here on the planet. My life is to be used in service to the awakening of humanity.

That might sound grandiose, but at ground zero, the everydayness of my life is quite ordinary. My life looks a lot like everyone else's, at least on the outside. But context is everything. It's the context from which we live that determines our experience.

My context is service. I'm here to serve my purpose wherever I am. In the checkout line at the grocery store, I can serve to help make someone's day a bit brighter. It only takes eye contact, a warm smile, and an open heart to make connections with people. You'd be surprised how willing people are to connect with strangers when they feel sincerity coming from the other person. Try it and see for yourself.

When I take care of my granddaughter, I am in service to her, to her mother, my daughter, to her father, my son-in-law, and to the universe. How blessed I feel getting to help raise this little being!

And then I get to travel to far off places in the world and lead seminars like the one I attended in 1975 and be a part of other people's journey of awakening. This too, serves my purpose and makes my life worth living. My life is about being in service to something greater than my own need for comfort.

Today, in my mid-seventies, I'm much closer to the finish line. Its increasing proximity puts a fine patina on the richness of whatever is left of my life. I feel a quickening, a knowing that while I may still have decades left to live, it becomes even more important that my remaining years be lived in service to my purpose. This is not the time to kick back and coast. Now post cancer scare, I have another chance at life, an opportunity to continue to make a difference. How will I use it?

I'm reminded of Mary Oliver's wonderful poem:

When Death Comes

When death comes like the hungry bear in autumn
when death comes and takes all the bright coins from his purse
to buy me, and snaps his purse shut;
when death comes like the measle-pox;
when death comes like an iceberg between the shoulder blades,
I want to step through the door full of curiosity, wondering;
what is it going to be like, that cottage of darkness?
And therefore I look upon everything
as a brotherhood and a sisterhood,
and I look upon time as no more than an idea,
and I consider eternity as another possibility,
and I think of each life as a flower,
as common as a field daisy, and as singular,
and each name a comfortable music in the mouth
tending as all music does, toward silence,

and each body a lion of courage, and something
precious to the earth.
When it's over, I want to say: all my life
I was a bride married to amazement.
I was a bridegroom, taking the world into my arms.
When it's over, I don't want to wonder
if I have made of my life something particular, and real.
I don't want to find myself sighing and frightened
or full of argument.
I don't want to end up simply having visited this world.

Each of us has a choice about how we live out our days in this lifetime. We can live in lockstep with our conditioning and never question if the choices we're making are our own or if we're just following the script. In which case, we'll end up, as Mary Oliver writes, "simply having visited this world."

On the surface, this might appear to be the easier approach. Follow the rules: don't make waves, please others, ignore your own feelings, keep a low profile, upset no one, be careful what you do and say, be concerned about what other people think of you, be in control at all times, avoid difficulties and anything unpleasant. Lots of people live this life and appear to do it well, at least on the surface.

I've worked with thousands of people over the years that have lived according to these unwritten rules for being human, and it's clear that while this life might appear to be working, it comes at a heavy price. The price? Knowing who you are, that's all. But that's everything. And it's a prescription for being stuck and lost. Perhaps a deeper source of fulfillment comes when we live in alignment with our higher purpose.

To live on purpose is to live a life that is sourced from the deep waters of the soul. Consider that the soul has its own agenda. Sooner or later, it will have its way with us. The soul comes to fulfill its purpose. The sooner one can discover that purpose and align with it, the more grace we experience in the journey.

A life lived "on purpose" is not automatically an easier life. There will be challenges ahead because you're not avoiding anything. Some of us come with strong and powerful lessons to complete. To live your life on purpose insures that you'll be on a continuous learning curve, taking new territory, dealing with uncertainty. When you align yourself with a larger purpose you are on a track supported by the process of life itself. You are here to fulfill your purpose.

Your purpose becomes your point of reference, your personal GPS. Choices that were obscure now become obvious. You operate from a level of Higher Being as opposed to being driven by the automatic, reactive, conditioned Ego. You learn to access your own wisdom and trust it. Imagination and intuition spark creative responses to life instead of automatic reactions. What once looked like a huge risk becomes the next obvious step toward your authentic life. You sense yourself moving toward "home", your deeper truth. Your dreams take form. This is a life lived with intention. This is a life lived "on purpose". To me, this is a life worth living.

Like Mary Oliver, I don't want to end up having simply visited this world. My purpose is to serve the planet in awakening to a higher consciousness. For over forty years, I've served my purpose through teaching, training, coaching, speaking and writing, being a mother, a grandmother, and a friend.

David Brooks, *New York Times* op-ed columnist and commentator on *PBS' News Hour*, wrote a column in the *Times*, called "The Summoned Self." In his column, Brooks discussed Clayton Christensen's *Harvard Business Review* essay on the "Well Planned Life", in which Christensen advised students to, early in life, invest time discovering their life's purpose and learn how to direct their time, energy and talents towards that end.

For Christensen, a well-planned life is plotted out much like a business strategy, using metrics and methodologies that take into account risks vs. rewards. The end "product" is a life that unfolds like a well-designed project: well thought out and crafted in the beginning, fine-tuned as needed along the way, and brought to a fruitful harvest.

The downside however, as Christensen points out, is that people who are high achievers often direct their energies towards those activities that will render the highest short-term rewards, like closing a sale or finishing a paper, and end up giving insufficient energy and attention to things like family and relationships, which don't produce an instant harvest.

Twenty years down the road, these people often discover their planning didn't include time for the things that ended up mattering most and they had misdirected their energies, a classic example of living from the head and ignoring the heart.

Brooks contrast this with what he calls "The Summoned Life":

"This mode of thinking starts from a different perspective. Life isn't a project to be completed; it is an unknowable landscape to be explored. A 24-year-old can't sit down and define the purpose of life in the manner of a school exercise because she is not yet deep enough into the landscape to know herself or her purpose. That young person – or any person – can't see into the future to know what wars, loves, diseases and chances may loom. She may know concepts, like parenthood or old age, but she doesn't understand their meanings until she is engaged in them."

For Brooks, the "summoned life" is one in which the context determines the content. The questions one asks are not "what is my purpose?" but rather "what is life asking of me, given my circumstances?"

A summoned life is created from one's heartfelt commitments to the things that matter most and where commitments to family, faith, nation or various causes are not made from balancing a ledger sheet. They emanate from the heart and often defy logic and cannot be quantified by traditional measures.

You might wonder, are these approaches mutually exclusive? Can't I plan my life and live it from my heart? The answer is as long as you understand that life doesn't always go according to plan or on our timeline or render the results we intended. There is no greater example of that than the times in which we live.

Due to economic conditions many people work far longer than they ever thought they would, have fewer retirement resources than they planned for, or find themselves out of work with dwindling opportunities to begin again. Many people today are not living the life they'd planned and are at the point where they believe there isn't enough time to fine tune and start over.

So much for the well-laid plan. I'm not against planning. Planning is good. Just don't mistake the plan for the real thing. Or as this line in the Swedish army manual says, "If the terrain and the map do not agree, follow the terrain".

Follow the terrain. The terrain, which is context, will tell you what comes next. If you're in a deep valley, bisected by a river with a strong flowing current, something different is being asked of you than if you find yourself at the top of a mountain, or floating down a lazy stream in a pontoon boat.

How we get from one terrain to another is the journey of life. You can make and execute well-crafted plans and they may get you where you want to go. But if you get blown off course, your plans will need to be changed or thrown out and a new course charted. As long as we use a plan more as a blueprint than a Bible, we have the freedom and flexibility to be innovative when the plan stops working.

If you don't listen to your heart, if you don't read what's written on it, the best laid plans will often deliver you to the wrong doorstep. How many people do you know prepared for a career because they hoped it would be the quickest way to riches and ended up leaving their chosen field because it wasn't compatible with who they were?

If you're not living the life you've planned, instead of panicking, consider that your life's circumstances, just the way they are, could be a blessing. You may discover that in losing what you told yourself you wanted, you instead found freedom. Upon closer examination, many people recognize their life plan wasn't theirs at all, but something they took on to live up to someone else's expectations. Whose life are you living?

You might think you don't have the luxury to follow your heart for guidance, but if you're struggling to find your way in these times, consider your circumstances are an invitation for you to reinvent yourself. So why not be inspired to create whatever's next based on the dreams you put away or set aside to pursue what no longer exists?

If life has taken you down a path you never intended to travel, take a glance around this new territory and check out the forest and the trees. Assume you're not here by accident but find yourself here for a reason. Consider what's possible, given what's so. Your life has brought you to this moment, so now what?

Food for Thought

- Knowing you will die someday, what do you see most important to fulfill in the life you have left to live?

- Can you see the path of your purpose? Are you on or off track?

- What steps do you need to take now to step into this life?

CHAPTER EIGHTEEN

Beyond the Box:
Wake Up and Live!

"Your time is limited, so don't waste it living someone else's life. Don't be trapped by dogma, which is living with the results of other people's thinking. Don't let the noise of others' opinions drown out your own inner voice. And most important, have the courage to follow your heart and intuition. They somehow already know what you truly want to become. Everything else is secondary."

Steve Jobs

After wandering through the desert of lost and stuck, spending time in confusion, hopelessness and self-doubt, and to quote Steve Jobs, "trapped by dogma and living the results of others' opinions," one day you notice a tiny ray of light piercing through the darkness.

In this small ray of light you can barely see the outline of a door. After looking for a way out for so long, you rub your eyes in disbelief. Could this be the opening you've been searching for? You head for the door, open it and are flooded with light. Guess what? You just woke up!

It's an interesting experience to wake up. Once awake, you find it hard to believe you were ever asleep. What was once obscured by uncertainty and fear now appears obvious to anyone who cared to look. Especially you.

You wonder, "How did I not see this before? What was I thinking that had me miss these obvious signs? It's all so clear now. How did I get so off track?"

Yes, that's the question, isn't it? Seen from the vantage point of being awake, the way ahead appears obvious now. As if any fool could have seen it. And yet, for all the reasons we've discussed in this book, you didn't.

The key right now is that you don't fall into blame and self-deprecation for being blinded for so long. We will get off track and lose ourselves time and time again over the course of a lifetime. It's called "being human" and it's part of the curriculum.

I've wandered in the desert of lost and stuck more times than I can count. I've spent years in the desert. Why did it take me so long to find my way out? I assert it was part of my soul's process. But I will tell you this: I did not emerge from any of my experiences as the same woman who went into them. I believe with all my heart that my soul led me down the paths I needed to go to get the lessons I needed to learn.

Even though the path was painful, it taught me life lessons I couldn't learn any other way. How do I know? Because it's what happened! If I could have learned these lessons some other way, I would have.

So here's the thing: life happens, and then you choose how you will respond. It sounds so simple, yet it's the one thing the majority of human beings fail to understand. They fail to see they have choice in the matter of their own lives.

By not seeing you have choice every moment, even in the lost and stuck moments, you give up your personal power and let fear take the wheel of your life. Here's the key to staying awake, staying found and staying on track: accept 100% responsibility for yourself and your life. No exceptions.

Why would anyone want to do that? Most people think of taking responsibility as equivalent to taking the blame. In most cultures, this is how responsibility has been defined. But in a context of transformation, responsibility has an entirely different meaning. Let's try this on for size:

Responsibility is a structure of interpretation wherein I declare myself to be the author of my life. This includes my thoughts, feelings, actions, interpretations and results. This is not true, like a fact. It's a choice I make.

Why would anyone make such a choice as this? It provides access to our personal power, freedom, aliveness and creativity. Spend time being a victim and see how powerful you feel. See how alive you feel. See how creative you are. There is no power in being a victim in life. As long as you remain a victim, you will remain lost.

So fine-tune your personal "radar" to detect when you start to go down the road of victim consciousness. You'll know it's happening when you blame someone or something else for your situation, or feelings. When you begin to think that "life is unfair," this shouldn't be happening, why is this happening to me," you have taken a turn down Victim Lane and you are headed straight towards the cliff.

Even when events over which you have no control happen in your life, you still are responsible for how you respond to them. You still have choice over your thoughts and feelings, once you've pulled yourself back from the abyss of victimhood.

The choice to be responsible is the quickest way to turn the corner from lost to found. This is the "brass ring"! This is what you've been searching for all along. You thought it was something outside yourself. But, no! It's your mental state, your beliefs, attitudes and opinions that determine if you're lost or stuck.

No matter what happens in the exterior world – you lose your job, your marriage ends, you lose all your money, a medical diagnosis – taking responsibility implies you have the ability to respond. It's a choice. It's not blame or guilt. Life happens and you choose how to respond. And that's all you need to stay in the lane called "awake".

When you accept responsibility, your actions will reflect that you, and not fear, are at the helm of your ship, driving your life. You won't always create the result you want and there is no guarantee you'll always come out on top. Take responsibility and choose again, and if necessary, again.

I was 34 years old when I first understood this concept. It was right before I took that seminar. In fact, this understanding is what got me into action and landed me in that room. I knew I had found the key I'd been missing for so long. It changed everything in my life.

I learned to face up to the unhappiness I felt in my marriage instead of being in denial about it and took responsibility for my role in it. Then I knew that it was I who needed to make the choice to end it. It was painful, because my husband was a good man and I loved him dearly, right up until the day he died. But he, being 15 years older than I, was more a father than a husband to me. I set it up to be that way. A father was exactly what I wanted. He provided the safety I needed at the time.

But after ten years of marriage, I was ready to be an adult and had to say the painful goodbye because my soul yearned to be free. It was the most difficult decision I've ever made in my life. Thirty years later, on the night he died, I was holding his hand, along with our two daughters.

I silently blessed him as he took his last breaths and asked him to forgive me for breaking his heart thirty years before. I think I heard him chuckle and tell me "you're free now, and so am I."

Some lessons come with higher price tags attached. You'll be required to pay the price if you want to get the lesson, so be prepared.

Waking up doesn't automatically mean that life is going to be easier because in truth, "awake, alive and free" is an even bigger game to play than "lost and asleep". Time spent there was a necessary part of the journey, but when you finally wake up you'll understand that the risks, challenges and rewards are much bigger.

You'll be faced with making bigger choices that will have bigger consequences. Sometimes you'll win and sometimes you'll lose. Don't be afraid to lose. You got here, so you must be big enough to play at this level. Life will give you the challenges you're big enough to meet, so sit up, grow up, pay attention, and get busy!

Here's an important lesson I've learned about staying awake. Surround yourself with a community of like-minded people who share a commitment to staying awake. Left to our own devices, it's too easy to fall back asleep. It requires a conscious effort and intention to stay awake and keep moving on the path of a purposeful life. You'll find other people who have that same intention. Buddy up with someone. Better yet, form a small group. Mastermind, brainstorm, coach each other. Find a coach who can support you to see what you can't and help keep you on track. Waking up doesn't happen all by itself. It's not a miracle. It's not magic. Waking up is what happens when you focus your intention and attention.

Find others who are creating big lives and who inspire you. Take notes. What do you see about them? What characteristics and qualities do they have in common? Pick one and arrange to interview them. Why not? My bet is they'd be thrilled and honored to support you.

One quality you'll most likely discover in people living extraordinary lives in the "Awake Lane" is they function from a clear vision and sense of purpose and part of the equation is to give back to others.

Chances are very high they've spent their fair share of time in the "Lost and Asleep" lane themselves and have gained much wisdom through their own experiences.

You'll be surprised to discover how willing they are to serve and mentor others who seek to be on the path along with them. So don't be afraid to ask for what you want! Let me say that again for it bears repeating: "Don't be afraid to ask for what you want!" If you don't ask, you'll never need to risk being rejected. But you'll never get to hear a "Yes" either!

You've got a big life waiting for you. I hope (there's that "hope" word) you live it full on, leave no stone unturned, so that when you get to the end, you can finish your life with a clear and peaceful heart. No regrets.

Food for Thought

- Now that you're awake, what possibilities do you see available to move your life ahead?

- Where are you going?

- What do you want?

- Go back to your 100-Day Challenge. Select a goal, and identify 3 limiting beliefs that have held you back. How will you overcome them?

- What inner resources do you have to support you?

- Don't forget to celebrate when you reach your goals. Pat yourself on the back and have a glass of champagne.

- Take notes and draw a map of how you got here. You're going to need it for the big challenges ahead. With faith and trust in yourself, knowing how far you've come, getting from "Lost" to "Awake" will become easier. The next time you find yourself at "Lost", you've got notes and a map to help you find your way back and remind you of what matters most.

CHAPTER NINETEEN

Your Calling is Calling

To find your calling is to find the intersection
between your own deep gladness, and the world's
deep hunger.

Steven Buebnor

There's a calling for your life you came to answer. It's your invitation for how and what you came to the planet to serve, the consciousness you came to represent. Do you know what it is?

If you don't know yet, it's your job to find out. Why? Because your calling is one that only *you* can answer. It was written on your soul when you arrived on this plane.

Consider that your soul took on a life in order for you find your calling and be its representative in the world. The work of your life is, and always has been, about preparing you to represent this calling. Your purpose is to discover and develop your ability to BE it, SPEAK it, and GIVE it away, for even as it is meant for you, it is not meant for you alone. Let's unpack this idea.

Your calling is about you being in service for the greater good of the whole. Discovering your calling is the key to you living the extraordinary and fulfilling life you came to live. Once you've leaned out, broken free, and risen up, it's time to find your unique expression of this calling and then take a stand for it and be its representative. Your calling propels you to speak who you are into the world. It has you blossom into being the fully self-expressed, self-actualized, abundant, radiant being you came to be.

The world is waiting for you. More than ever the world needs you.

Many people have shared with me their sense of despair over the current political and social realities in the U.S. and around the world. Some have lost their sense of hope and their conviction that being committed to creating a world that works for everyone can ever manifest in reality. "It's a nice sounding fantasy, but can it ever really happen?" They're ready to resign their former passionate stand for humanity and give up their dreams.

To them I say this:

There was never a time when the likes of you and your callings were more needed. Your stand for humanity, your passion about and commitment to making a difference for the world are more necessary now than ever before.

It is no accident that you and I are the ones here on planet Earth at the beginning of a new millennium. It is precisely this time for which we came.

The context of humanity is being shifted as we speak. We are in that part of the process that appears to be dark and treacherous. The box has been blown up and we are here in the darkness and chaos, attempting to find our bearings and the ground upon which we'll stand to create whatever is next.

Whatever is next is up to us. We can give up, lose hope, and descend into our own darkness. We can shrink and shrivel into a tiny version of our former selves. We can recreate the old box out of the rubble and crawl back inside and pretend that nothing has changed.

But my friend, if we did that, we would be in serious disillusionment. More than ever before in my 76 years on the planet, I am clear that now is the time for us to radiate ever brighter, to illuminate the darkness with our inner light. We must walk the talk we've talked for so long.

It's easy to walk the talk *when it's easy*. Anyone can do that. The question is: can you walk the talk when it's difficult? Can you walk the talk when it looks like there is no ground to walk on? Can you still be a stand for what matters most to you, when it looks like it no longer matters and no one cares? Can you still be a messenger of your message when you feel drowned out by the noise of chaos?

This is a time of reckoning for us humans. Who we become in these times will determine the quality of life we leave behind for our great-great-great grandchildren. We are the ancestors they will refer back to when they speak about what happened during this time in history. What's the legacy you're committed to leaving behind for them?

Your personal growth and development matters greatly, not only for your own sense of fulfillment and satisfaction, but also for the legacy you will create for your descendants. If you come from a lineage of addiction or abuse, if you come from a lineage of unworthiness, scarcity, fear or dishonesty, you can be the one who changes your entire lineage by "leaning out, breaking free, rising up" and daring to venture beyond that old box into a life that you create based on your vision and calling, not on automatic behaviors based on the past.

Your commitment to your own life requires that you do the work of breaking free of the past, your own and the one you inherited from those who came before.

The Native American tribe, Lakota Sioux, believe that our actions affect seven generations in both directions. If this is true, then it suggests that you can heal the wounds of your ancestors as well as change the future for those who come after you in your lineage. Think about this. When you shift, your entire lineage shifts with you.

I once had a dream about this. In the dream, I was standing before a long table. Seated at the table was what I call "the Ascended Masters". They were luminous beings. I couldn't see their faces in the dream, but I could hear their voices. Before me on the ground, was a line. The Ascended Masters said to me, "If you choose to cross this line, you will bring with you your entire lineage. The choice is yours."

As the voice spoke to me in the dream, I could see behind me a line of beings, all of which had their hands on the shoulders of the one in front of them. It was an endless chain of ancestral Beings, all connected to one another, with me being the one at the head of the line. There were hands on my shoulders as well. I could feel the energetic connection of the others, all flowing through them to me.

I responded to the call from the Masters and in the dream, I chose to step across the line. At that moment, I could feel a surge of energy rushing forward through my body, moving across with me. And then, I woke up.

I not only woke up physically, something else in me awakened. The dream was a message for me. I believe it was for me to get the importance of the kind of healing work I've done for over four decades and the impact on the collective. I got the message that we are the healers for past, present and future generations, IF we choose to free ourselves from the confinement of our conditioning, dare to go Beyond the Box and resolve to Lean Out, Break Free, and Rise Up!

This book is my contribution to the elevation of our collective awareness around this important work. I sincerely hope that you, dear reader, found something of value here. I welcome your feedback and questions. I can be reached through my website: www.judithrich.com.

Endnotes

While you may be almost finished with this book, the real work is about to begin. No more hiding out in your old stories, reasons and excuses for staying stuck or remaining lost. It's time to begin doing the uncomfortable work of actually confronting yourself and dismantling the stories you've been using to cling to whatever spot you've been clinging to "up until now". And those last three words, "up until now" are the key.

Your life is the way it's been "up until now". But that doesn't mean it needs to continue to be that way going forward. The work ahead requires that you be willing to explode your box, let go of those old stories and limiting beliefs you've held on to, and venture out beyond your current boundaries. Out beyond what you can currently see or know, lies a new field of possibilities waiting to be discovered. The only way you can access these new possibilities and bring them into form is through your belief in yourself, and 100% commitment to manifesting the life you want to live. Regardless of what may come up and appear to be obstacles, obstacles are merely life's way of inviting you to play a bigger game.

There is nothing in the way except your self-imposed limitations. While this may not be news to you, there's a difference between knowing something intellectually, and actually going for it.

So I say go for it! Go for it with everything you have. Go for it with your whole heart and soul. Swing for the fences. The worst that can happen is you miss the mark. But in the process you will have learned some mighty lessons. And next time around, you'll either hit the mark or get a lot closer. After all, life is the classroom in which we're following the curriculum we came to learn. By declaring yourself as a life-long learner, you'll be in learning mode from here on.

As a life-long learner, you "get" to take on the ups and downs with gusto and with faith in yourself and your ability to handle them. On one level, you are already "there". And what is "there", you ask? It's that place you call "found". Found is the place inside of you that's always been there. Just like Dorothy looking for that place called "home", only to discover it was in her all along. "Found" is the place in your Being that has always known who and where you are. It's your true North, the place in you that has always been aligned with your Highest Self.

The next time you venture out into new territory, be sure to stay awake and aligned with your vision and higher purpose. True up to them, like a compass that always points north. They will lead you on a journey of life-long learning and adventure. And when you reach the end of your days, you will look back on your life and be able to say "well done" and have no regrets.

As the South Africans say when they meet each other on the path, "Sawubona", meaning "we see you", so to you I say, "Sawubona". May your journey be filled with adventure. May you live a big, juicy, creative, uncomfortable life!

I leave you with another very beautiful poem by Mary Oliver:

"The Journey"

One day you finally knew
what you had to do, and began,
though the voices around you
kept shouting
their bad advice –
though the whole house
began to tremble
and you felt the old tug
at your ankles.
"Mend my life!"
each voice cried.
But you didn't stop.
You knew what you had to do,
though the wind pried
with its stiff fingers
at the very foundations,
though their melancholy
was terrible.
It was already late
enough, and a wild night,
and the road full of fallen
branches and stones.
But little by little,
as you left their voices behind,
the stars began to burn
through the sheets of clouds,
and there was a new voice

which you slowly
recognized as your own,
that kept you company
as you strode deeper and deeper
into the world,
determined to do
the only thing you could do –
determined to save
the only life you could save.

About The Author

Dr. Judith Rich is a pioneering teacher in the field of transformation and consciousness. She is an accomplished transformational and personal effectiveness trainer with over forty years' experience in training design, facilitation, executive coaching, organizational transformation and public speaking.

Her work is focused on the awakening of one's dormant inner resources, empowering profound personal and professional breakthroughs for thousands of individuals and organizations throughout the United States, Russia, Asia, Mexico and South America. As a speaker, writer, trainer, workshop facilitator and leadership development coach, Judith brings insight, passion, humor, sensitivity and wisdom to empower people's awakening to the brilliance of who they are.

"I believe that each human being has within, the seeds of his or her own greatness. We've simply forgotten who we are. Our job is to remember ourselves. Most of us struggle to fulfill our potential out of fear that we're not enough. We fail to see or believe in who we can be out of our unconscious, automatic conditioning that reinforces belief in our limitations. To accept who we are at the level of our highest Self is the work we've come to the planet to complete. From there, the only thing left to do is to give our gifts away and be willing to receive the abundance awaiting us. To live from our greatness is to accept responsibility for championing the greatness in others."

Dr. Judith Rich

With BA and MA degrees from Western Michigan University in Kalamazoo, MI, Judith began her career as a special education teacher, working with children and their parents to help unlock the potential of those with the biggest challenges. She received her Ph.D. from the Avalon Institute in Boulder, CO in 1995. She has been a featured contributor at the Huffington Post since 2008.

Dr. Rich lives in the San Francisco Bay area. A mother and grandmother, in addition to her coaching and training work, she enjoys reading, hiking, music, writing and spending time with her family.

For personal contact she may be reached at: judith@judithrich.com. To learn more about doing personal work with her, or book her for a speaking engagement, visit her website – www.judithrich.com.

References

Bach, Richard. *Jonathan Livingston Seagull*. New York, NY: Macmillan, 1971.

Brooks, David. "The Summoned Self." *New York Times*, August 3, 2010. Accessed April 5, 2018. URL.

Christensen, Clayton M. "How Will You Measure Your Life?" *Harvard Business Review*, July-August 2010. Accessed April 5, 2018. www.hbr.org.

Estes, Dr. Clarissa Pinkola. *Women Who Run With The Wolves*. New York, NY: Ballentine Books, 1996.

Ferguson, Marilyn. *Aquarian Conspiracy*. New York, NY: Tarcher, 1980.

Hillman, James. *The Soul's Code: In Search of Character and Calling*. New York, NY: Grand Central Publishing, 1999.

Oliver, Mary. *Poems: When Death Comes. The Journey*. Accessed April 6, 2018. http://www.famouspoetsandpoems.com/poets/mary_oliver/poems/15794.

Petit, Phillippe. Movie: Man On Wire! Directed by James Marsh. Discovery Films. 2008.

"The 2017 CNBC 50 Disruptor Companies", CNBC, 05/16/2017.

Accessed April 6, 2018. https://www.cnbc.com/2017/05/16/the-2017-cnbc-disruptor-50-list-of-companies.html.

"The Science of Gratitude: More Benefits Than Expected; 26 Studies and Counting". Happier Human: What About Happiness? Accessed April 4, 2018. www.happierhuman.com.

Suggested Readings

Beck, Martha. *Finding Your Own North Star*. New York, NY: Three Rivers Press, 2001.

Browne, Sylvia. *Soul's Perfection*. Carlsbad, CA: Hay House, 2000.

Cameron, Julia. *The Artist's Way*. New York, NY: Jeremy P. Tarcher/ Putnam Books, 1992

Chodron, Pema. *When Things Fall Apart*. Boston, Massachusetts: Shambhala, 1997.

Hillman, James. *The Soul's Code: In Search of Character and Calling*. New York, NY: Random House, 1996.

Nepo, Mark. *The One Life We're Given*. New York, NY: Atria Book, 2016.

McTaggart, Lynne. *The Intention Experiment*. New York, NY: Free Press, 2007.

Mohr, Tara. *Playing Big: Find Your Voice, Your Mission, Your Message*. New York, NY: Gotham Books, 2014.

Moore, Thomas. *Care of the Soul*. New York, NY: Harper Collins, 1992.

Muller, Wayne. *How Then, Shall We Live?* New York, NY: Bantam Books, 1996.

Sandberg, Sheryl. *Lean In: Women, Work, and the Will to Lead*. New York, NY: Alfred Knopf, 2014.

Siefer, Nancy and Vieweg, Martin. *When The Soul Awakens*. Reston, VA: Gathering Waves Press, 2009.

Tolle, Eckhart. *The Power of Now*. Novato, CA: New World Library, 1999.

81972278R10102

Made in the USA
San Bernardino, CA
13 July 2018